# ORTHO'S All Ab

# Azaleas,
## Camellias & Rhododendrons

Written by H. Edward Reiley

Meredith® Books

Ortho® Books
An imprint of Meredith® Books

**All About Azaleas, Camellias & Rhododendrons**
Writer: H. Edward Reiley
Editor: Marilyn Rogers
Technical Consultant: Harold E. Greer
Art Director: Tom Wegner
Assistant Art Director: Harijs Priekulis
Copy Chief: Catherine Hamrick
Copy and Production Editor: Terri Fredrickson
Book Production Managers: Pam Kvitne,
    Marjorie J. Schenkelberg
Contributing Copy Editors: Chardel Gibson Blaine,
    Elizabeth Neils, Angela K. Renkoski, Barbara Feller-Roth
Contributing Proofreaders: Sue Fetters, Joseph E. Irwin,
    Barbara J. Stokes, JoEllyn Witke
Contributing Prop/Photo Stylist: Peggy Johnston
Indexer: Donald Glassman
Electronic Production Coordinator: Paula Forest
Editorial and Design Assistants: Kathleen Stevens,
    Karen Schirm

**Additional Editorial Contributions from**
    **Art Rep Services**
Director: Chip Nadeau
Designer: lk Design
Illustrator: Dave Brandon

**Meredith® Books**
Editor in Chief: James D. Blume
Design Director: Matt Strelecki
Managing Editor: Gregory H. Kayko
Executive Ortho Editor: Larry Erickson

Director, Retail Sales and Marketing: Terry Unsworth
Director, Sales, Special Markets: Rita McMullen
Director, Sales, Premiums: Michael A. Peterson
Director, Sales, Retail: Tom Wierzbicki
Director, Sales, Home & Garden Centers: Ray Wolf
Director, Book Marketing: Brad Elmitt
Director, Operations: George A. Susral
Director, Production: Douglas M. Johnston

Vice President, General Manager: Jamie L. Martin

**Meredith Publishing Group**
President, Publishing Group: Christopher M. Little
Vice President, Finance & Administration: Max Runciman

**Meredith Corporation**
Chairman and Chief Executive Officer: William T. Kerr

Chairman of the Executive Committee: E.T. Meredith III


H. Edward Reiley is president of the International
Rhododendron Society. Harold E. Greer is owner of
Greer Gardens Nursery.

**Thanks to**
Janet Anderson, Kathy Roth Eastman, Karin Holms,
    Colleen Johnson

**Photographers**
(Photographers credited may retain copyright ©
    to the listed photographs.)
L = Left, R = Right, C = Center, B = Bottom, T = Top
**William D. Adams:** 45TR, 47BR; **APS Press:** 45Inset;
**Kate Boykin:** 62R; **Barbara Bullock/U. S. National
Arboretum:** 46L, 47BL, 81L; **Rob Cardillo:** 28, 30-3, 30-4,
30-5, 32T, 32B, 40T, 40C, 40B, 41TL, 41TC, 41TR, 41BL,
41BC, 41BR; **R. Todd Davis:** 66T; **Brian Durell:** 63L;
**Derek Fell:** 6; **Flowerwood:** 12; **John Glover:** 55B, 89;
**David Goldberg:** 29T; **Harold E. Greer:** 19, 43TR, 44R,
56BR, 57B; **Jerry Harpur:** 21B, 52B, 63R; **Marcus Harpur:**
54T, 60T; **Lynne Harrison:** 48R, 88B; **Saxon Holt:** 9T, 9C,
9B, 53T, 55T, 58B, 88T; **Dency Kane:** 8C, 51T, 56T, 77;
**Dick Keen/Visuals Unlimited:** 71T, 72T; **Donna & Tom
Krischan:** 13, 14B, 25BR, 79B; **Michael Landis:** 57T;
**Andrew Lawson:** 15L, 17BC, 17BR, 82B; **Janet Loughrey:**
24, 44L, 48L, 49, 54B, 83L; **Julie Maris/Semel:** 79T; **Stuart
McCall:** 4T, 20, 23T, 25T; **Bryan McCay:** 30-2; **Monrovia:**
91, 91B; **J. Paul Moore:** 7; **Clive Nichols:** 23B, 85, 86R,
87B, 90; **Jerry Pavia:** 11B, 51B, 65L, 70, 71B, 73, 74T, 74B,
81R, 82T; **Pam Peirce:** 46TR; **Gary W. Moorman/
Pennsylvania State University:** 46BR; **Ben Phillips/Positive
Images:** 8B, 11T, 66B, 72B, 75, 78T, 84; **Richard Shiell:**
4BL, 10, 16, 17TL, 17TC, 17TR, 21T, 43L, 50, 53B, 61T,
64, 83T, 83B, 86L, 87T; **Pam Spaulding/Positive Images:**
8T, 22, 59B; **Donald Specker:** 45TL; **Albert
Squillace/Positive Images:** 80L; **Steve Struse:** 30-1, 35, 42;
**The Studio Central:** 29B; **Michael S. Thompson:** 4BR,
14T, 15R, 17BL, 18, 27, 43 BR, 44Inset, 45BL, 47T, 52T,
56BL, 59T, 60B, 61B, 62L, 65R, 67T, 68T, 68B, 69T, 69B,
76T, 76B, 80R; **Connie Toops:** 67B, 78B

On the cover: 'Trude Webster' rhododendron. Photograph by
    Michael S. Thompson.

All of us at Ortho® Books are dedicated to providing you
with the information and ideas you need to enhance your
home and garden. We welcome your comments and
suggestions about this book. Write to us at:
    Meredith Corporation
    Ortho Books
    1716 Locust St.
    Des Moines, IA 50309–3023

If you would like more information on other Ortho products,
call 800-225-2883 or visit us at www.ortho.com

**Note to the Readers:** Due to differing conditions, tools,
and individual skills, Meredith Corporation assumes no
responsibility for any damages, injuries suffered, or losses
incurred as a result of following the information published
in this book. Always read and observe all of the safety
precautions provided by manufacturers of any tools,
equipment, or supplies, and follow all accepted
safety procedures.

# INTRODUCING AZALEAS, RHODODENDRONS, & CAMELLIAS 4

# GROWING RHODODENDRONS, AZALEAS & CAMELLIAS 24

# ENCYCLOPEDIA OF RHODODENDRONS, AZALEAS & CAMELLIAS 48

Rhododendrons line a
walk in a Vancouver
botanical garden.

Rhododendron *'Trude Webster'*
provides a restful backdrop in a
secluded corner of the garden.

*This winter-blooming camellia adds color,
grace, and beauty to the garden.*

# INTRODUCING AZALEAS, RHODODENDRONS & CAMELLIAS

This trio of prized ornamental shrubs graces landscapes the world over. Each has a signature characteristic: Azaleas are renowned for their vibrant displays of color, rhododendrons for their spectacular and dramatic flower clusters, and camellias for their perfectly formed, iridescent blossoms.

Because these plants grow in a variety of shapes and sizes and boast handsome foliage with diverse textures, their versatility in the landscape—from woodland settings to beds, borders, and containers—is virtually unmatched. They tend to be long-lived plants so they make reliable permanent plantings. Their showy flowers and dramatic bold foliage also make them striking design features.

Rhododendrons and azaleas come from a distinctly different plant family than camellias, but the three are similar in many respects. For that reason, azaleas, rhododendrons, and camellias are sometimes discussed together in this book because their cultural requirements and landscape uses are similar. At other times they are treated separately because of differences in their history, adaptability, and physical characteristics of size and development, leaf texture, and flower type.

Similarities include the fact that they all relish moist, slightly acid, humus-rich, well-drained soil, and require some shade for best performance. They grow best near established trees that provide afternoon shade. In new developments where trees are small or non-existent, the shadows of buildings or other structures are acceptable substitutes.

From a distance, the three even look alike with their glossy, dark green leaves and shrubby habit. As a rule, they look good together and complement many other plantings.

The largest concentration of native species of these three shrubs is in a triangle of Asia, including Nepal, parts of southwestern China, and northern Burma. In particular, the provinces of Yunnan and Sichuan in western China are treasuries of rhododendron and camellia species.

Hybridizers have used many of these species as breeding stock for exciting new hybrids. Combined with superior selections of the species, these new hybrids add color to the landscape while requiring less care. Extending the range of cold hardiness is still a concern, but the quality of hybrid offspring continues to improve as breeders find new species, better forms of already known species, and newly discovered natural hybrids to work with. In particular, the genus Rhododendron offers such a plethora of diverse characteristics that there appears no end to the new releases that may one day populate the world's gardens.

# RHODODENDRONS & AZALEAS

**Rhododendron ponticum** *is native to the Caucasus and northern Turkey, where it often dominates the landscape. It grows from sea level to 6,000 feet.*

A few rhododendrons have been in cultivation for centuries, but azaleas have the richest and longest history. In fact, the first record of deciduous azaleas dates back to the 4th century B.C., when honey from *Rhododendron luteum* poisoned thousands of Greek soldiers retreating from Persia.

Azaleas were first mentioned in Japanese poetry in A.D. 759. Since that time, the Japanese have kept a revered place for these finely textured and delicate plants in their gardens, thought, and lore.

## AZALEAS ON THE MOVE

Early Buddhist monks brought Japanese azaleas to China and Asia. Plant collectors then introduced azaleas to Europe. Many of these were cultivated plants collected from gardens in China and Japan and may have been hybrids rather than species taken from the wild. Although this fact has little bearing on how people grow and use the plants, the

distinction is important to botanists and hybridizers. Because the offspring of species are more likely to be predictable than the offspring of hybrids, knowing the origin helps determine which plants to use when breeding new cultivars.

Azaleas also arrived in Europe from the New World. The azalea *R. viscosum* was first grown in England in 1680 from seed collected in Virginia. In the 1870s, outstanding American plantsman John Bartram introduced three North American azalea species—*R. viscosum*, *R. periclymenoides*, and *R. calendulaceum*—to England. English hybridizers bred these native American species with tender azalea species to impart cold hardiness to the offspring.

The majority of evergreen azaleas originated in Japan, where the first attempts at hybridizing occurred. Europe received its first evergreen azaleas in the 20th century. They came into prominence in 1918 when plant explorer E. H. Wilson introduced 50 Kurume azalea cultivars (see page 10) from Japan. These Kurumes were later imported into the United States.

One of the most important azalea introductions to the United States was *R. kaempferi*. In 1892, Professor Charles S. Sargent of the Arnold Arboretum in Massachusetts imported this very cold-hardy species, which ultimately was responsible for extending the landscape use of evergreen azaleas into the colder areas of the eastern United States. Some of the hybrids that resulted from crosses with this species produce flower buds that are hardy to −15° F, and many species are still available today.

## RHODODENDRONS

By comparison, most rhododendrons have been in cultivation for a relatively short period of time. The first rhododendron species—*R. hirsutum*—was introduced from the wild in 1653. England received the North American species, *R. maximum*, and numerous other azalea species in 1736. However, the bulk of new introductions occurred in the early 20th century from Asia. These striking plants stirred the imagination of plant collectors, many of whom mounted daring expeditions in search of new varieties. Expeditions to Asia and the Himalayas brought back many new, exciting species and a wealth of materials to use in hybridizing.

Three of the most notable 20th-century plant explorers were E. H. Wilson, George Forest, and F. Kingdon-Ward. Wilson sent back 40 new species of rhododendron from China between 1900 and 1902. Forest introduced 260 species starting in 1904 and Kingdon-Ward 100 species starting in 1911.

The first planned hybridizing of rhododendrons began in England in 1810. Washington, D.C., received its first hybrid rhododendrons in the 1860s, and the first commercially popular rhododendron hybrids arrived in the United States in 1876. Known as the Iron Clads because of their ease of culture, they soon became popular and widely distributed. Many of these Iron Clad hybrids are still on the market.

The search for new rhododendron species continues primarily in Asia. Today, prominent explorers from Scotland, the United States, and other countries actively explore Asia in search of new species and improved specimens of previously introduced species.

## NATIVE HABITATS

The world's highest mountain range, the Himalayas, stretches more than 1,500 miles in a great arc across the top of India. With a wide range of microclimates, the Himalayas are home to a remarkable variety of plants. Tropical rain forests thrive on the lower slopes, where exotic tree ferns and orchids flourish. At higher elevations, the landscape changes to treeless snow ridges and alpine meadows, where only the hardiest plants survive.

Two-thirds of the world's 800-plus rhododendron species grow between 2,000 and 18,000 feet of altitude. Shrouded in mist for much of the year, the valleys are host to tree rhododendrons, which grow to monstrous proportions under these ideal conditions. Kingdon-Ward, one of the most determined plant explorers, while crisscrossing the Himalayas in the 1920s and 1930s described a rhododendron on the Tibetan-Burmese frontier as 55 feet high with a 6-foot-diameter trunk. It bore 800 soccer-ball-size trusses of shimmering red flowers.

At 8,000 feet, rhododendrons are so thick and tall that they dominate the ecosystem. At 12,000 to 18,000 feet, where the conifer forest gives way to scrub, rhododendrons become prostrate with small flowers, more like the heaths and heathers to which they are related. Here, the plants—many of them with narrow leaves and strong fragrance—carpet the ground for miles.

Tropical climates, notably New Guinea, Malaysia, and the Philippines, are the native home to large numbers of rhododendron species, including many vireyas. There is also an indigenous Australian species.

Rhododendrons have not been found in either Africa or South America, but a few species did originate in Europe, particularly in the Alps. North America has a significant number of native species—around 20—including many azaleas.

R. maximum, *the rosebay rhododendron, is a large-growing species native to the eastern United States. Like this species, a great number of rhododendrons originated in misty, mountainous regions.*

# DISTINCTIONS

Azaleas: Single flowers cover their branches. Leaves are small, thin, light green, and rounded.

Lepidotes: Plants have small trusses at branch tips. This is 'P.J.M.', a very cold-hardy lepidote.

Elepidotes: Large, ball-shaped trusses at the ends of branches and large, leathery leaves mark elepidote rhododendrons. This elepidote is 'Cunningham White'.

More than 800 species of plants in the genus *Rhododendron* and about 17,000 cultivars are currently registered with the Royal Horticultural Society. Of these, 97 are azalea species and 7,112 are azalea hybrids. Another 9,107 are rhododendron hybrids, 303 are rhododendron species, 18 vireya species, 417 vireya hybrids, and 73 are azaleodendrons (hybrids having an azalea parent and a rhododendron parent). Because the classification of the genus is extremely complex and constantly changing as research reveals new relationships between groups, these numbers or classifications are subject to change.

When the great plantsman Linnaeus began his famous system of plant classification, he placed azaleas and rhododendrons in separate genera. Later, taxonomists decided that they belong together. Today, gardeners and the nursery industry find it easier and clearer to make distinctions between the two plants.

## MAJOR DIFFERENCES

In many cases, the differences between azaleas and rhododendrons are readily apparent. Azaleas have small leaves and profuse flowers scattered over the entire shrub. The leaves of rhododendrons are leathery, and the flowers are in large clusters at the ends of the stems.

However, distinctions between the two groups are not always perfectly defined. For example, both azaleas and lepidote rhododendrons have small leaves. Where they differ is on the undersides of their leaves. Lepidote leaves are covered in tiny scales; azaleas have no scales. Also, the leaves of rhododendrons tend to be thicker, darker green and more robust appearing.

Regarding flowers, individual blossoms of azaleas are generally smaller than those of rhododendrons, even those of some lepidotes. But seen en masse, their blossoms are just as impressive.

## HYBRIDIZING

Although azaleas and rhododendrons are the same species and there are such hybrids as azaleodendrons, for the most part they don't make good breeding partners. Few of the resulting hybrids have much landscape value. However, hybridizing within the two groups has produced many new varieties.

In particular, native American rhododendrons have been crossed with tender Himalayan rhododendrons to produce highly desirable colors in hardy offspring that are suitable for some of the coldest climates. (Both azaleas and North American rhododendrons are much more cold-hardy than most of their Asian counterparts.)

## HOW TO TELL RHODODENDRONS FROM AZALEAS

### AZALEAS

■ Azalea leaves are usually small, narrow, and pointed.
■ The undersides of leaves usually have small hairs, especially along the midrib. Also, azalea leaves are thinner, softer, and easier to bend than those of rhododendrons.
■ Flowers are usually flatter than those of large-leaf rhododendrons.
■ Flowers are borne along the sides and on the tips of the stems. They develop individually or in clusters.
■ Flowers have five lobes.
■ Flowers usually have five stamens.

### RHODODENDRONS

■ Elepidotes have large, broad, long, leathery leaves that are blunt at the tips.
■ Leaves of some lepidotes are smaller than azalea leaves. Even so, the leaves of most lepidotes are heavier in texture, usually hairless, and not as pointed at the tips. Scales coat leaf undersides.
■ Flowers are more bell-shaped and usually larger than azalea flowers.
■ Flowers are borne in trusses—large clusters of individual blossoms—at the ends of branches.
■ Flowers may have five to seven lobes.
■ Flowers often have 10 or more stamens.

## TERMINOLOGY

Rhododendron, azalea, and camellia growers use specialized terms when discussing these plants. Here are a few of the most common.

### RHODODENDRONS

**LEPIDOTE:** With scales. It refers to a group of rhododendrons with tiny scales on the undersides of the leaves.

**ELEPIDOTE:** Without scales. Elepidote denotes a group of rhododendrons having no scales on the leaf undersides.

**INDUMENTUM:** The wooly or hairy covering on the undersides of the leaves of some rhododendrons. Indumentum is particularly noticeable on R. *yakushimanum*.

### PLANTS

**DECIDUOUS:** A plant that drops its leaves cyclically.

**EVERGREEN:** A plant maintaining at least a portion of its leaves year-round.

**EPIPHYTE:** A plant that grows on another plant or object but is nonparasitic. It derives nutrients from air, rainwater, and organic matter in the crotches and other cavities or under the bark of trees.

### FLOWERS

**PETAL:** A modified leaf, which is often brightly colored.

**PETALOID:** Resembling a petal. In these plants, stamens become petaloid and create double flowers.

**COROLLA:** A flower.

**SINGLE:** A flower with one row of petals.

**DOUBLE:** Having more than two rows of petals; may be as fully petaled as a peony.

**HOSE-IN-HOSE:** A flower appearing to have two corollas superimposed on each other.

**TRUSS:** The large cluster of flowers of a rhododendron.

**BLOTCH:** A darker-colored spot that may occur on the top, upright petal of some rhododendron flowers.

**DEADHEADING:** Removing spent flowers to prevent seed set.

### PARENTAGE TERMS

**SPECIES:** Distinct groups of recognizable plants that interbreed freely among themselves. Species evolve in isolation. Under such conditions they tend to become more and more alike as they inbreed within the group. The plants that are genetically best adapted to local growing conditions survive; plants not adapted die off. The result is a uniform group of plants adapted to a specific environment. Species are genetically more homogeneous than hybrids; therefore, they are more alike than groups of hybrids.

**HYBRID:** A plant developed through cross-breeding. It can result from a cross between two species, a hybrid and a species, or two hybrids. Hybrids in the wild are the result of cross-pollination between two different species. The resulting hybrids are genetically more heterogeneous than their parents. They show more physical differences and are therefore more variable as a group than are species. They are also usually more vigorous and more widely adapted to varying climatic conditions.

**CLONE:** A plant that is genetically identical to its parents.

**CULTIVAR:** Traditionally a contraction of "cultivated variety." All plants carrying a cultivar name are genetically identical and exhibit the same physical characteristics. When asexually reproduced, cultivars retain their physical characteristics and are exact duplicates of the parent plant.

**VARIETY:** A naturally occurring variation of a wild species. Varieties are given names to indicate their separate identity. For example, R. *thomsonii pallida* is the sole variety of the species R. *thomsonii*. Variety is often used in the same way as cultivar.

**SPORT:** A spontaneous plant mutation. It usually appears as a shoot having flowers or foliage different from the rest of the plant.

### SOIL

**FLOCCULATION:** The clumping together of soil particles to form larger masses. Soil structure is improved through flocculation.

**LEACH:** To wash plant nutrients out of the soil.

**PH:** A measure of soil acidity or alkalinity. pH 7 is neutral. Numbers above 7 indicate alkalinity, below 7 indicate acidity. Most plants grow best in a slightly acid soil. Azaleas, camellias, and rhododendrons grow best at pH 5 to 6. Each unit of change, such as from pH 5 to 6, represents 10 times the acidity or alkalinity of the previous unit.

*Elepidote rhododendrons often have relatively large leaves with no scales on the undersides of their leaves.*

*Lepidote rhododendrons generally have smaller, narrower leaves with tiny dot-like scales on the undersides.*

*Indumentum means hairy, and this 'Ken Janeck' rhododendron demonstrates it well.*

# AZALEAS

*Evergreen azaleas such as this 'Red Bird' provide a beautiful background for low-growing primroses.*

Azaleas are divided into two categories: evergreen and deciduous. The most visible difference between the two groups is the longevity of their leaves. Although evergreen azaleas have leaf growth cycles when they lose leaves, they do keep some leaves throughout the year. Deciduous azaleas shed their leaves as they go through the annual period of dormancy. Within both groups, azaleas are subdivided into either azalea species or azalea hybrids. The hybrids are further broken down into hybrid groups.

## EVERGREEN AZALEAS

Evergreen azaleas are easily distinguishable by their leaves. Although healthy evergreen azaleas normally keep their leaves year-round, their leaves do change with the seasons.

In colder climates, evergreen azaleas lose some leaves, and in extreme cold they can lose all of their leaves. Evergreen azaleas' spring leaves are thinner, lighter, and larger than their summer leaves which turn yellow and fall off in drought conditions and in autumn. This is a natural phenomenon and need not cause alarm. Summer leaves are crowded near the top of the branch, and they are generally thicker and smaller than spring leaves; they remain attached to the plant throughout the dormant period.

The leaves of different varieties of evergreen azaleas also vary depending on their flower color. White-flowering evergreen azaleas have light green leaves in summer and show little if any fall color change. Pink-, red-, or purple-flowering plants have darker summer leaves and develop bright fall colors of red or purple. This leaf color can help identify plants when they are not in bloom.

## HYBRIDS

Evergreen hybrid azaleas are divided into 20 groups named for the parent plants, the hybridizer, or the nursery that developed them. Many of the most popular evergreen azalea hybrids are derived from species native to eastern Asia. By custom, the hybrid groups are arranged, as in the list that follows, according to the order in which they were introduced to this country.

■ **BELGIAN INDIAN, OR RUTHERFORD, HYBRIDS:** Development of the Belgian Indian, or simply Belgian, hybrids began in the early 1800s in Europe, mainly in Belgium and England. Rutherfords are their American counterpart. These hybrids vary considerably in size, flower color, and hardiness. Breeders are currently working with them to develop greenhouse plants with semidouble to double ruffled flowers for forcing.

■ **SOUTHERN INDIAN, OR INDICA, HYBRIDS:** Southern Indian hybrids (sometimes known as Southern Indicas) are generally large plants with large flowers. They are common in the Deep South. They tolerate more hot sun than the Belgian Indians. Most suffer considerable damage at temperatures below 10° F.

■ **KURUME HYBRIDS:** Kurume azaleas are among the most popular of the hybrid groups. The most important parent of the Kurumes is *R. sataense,* an isolated species from the island of Kyushu in southern Japan. Kurumes are hardier than Southern Indians and slower growing, but they will grow to 5 feet tall or more. In early spring, they bear profusely, the small flowers ranging in color from white to pink, orange, red, and purple. Plants are hardy to −5° to −10° F.

■ **KAEMPFERI HYBRIDS:** Kaempferi hybrids are crosses of *R. kaempferi* and *R.* 'Malvatica', a clone of unknown parentage from Holland. Many of the Kaempferi hybrids are vigorous and tall, often reaching 8 feet or more, with an upright growth habit. They are hardy to −10° F. In cold regions, Kaempferi azaleas are nearly deciduous in winter. Depending on the cultivar, they bear 1½- to 2½-inch-wide reddish-orange, pink to purple, or white single or hose-in-hose flowers in midseason.

■ **GABLE HYBRIDS:** Many of the hybrids that resulted from the work of hybridizer Joseph B. Gable were crosses of *R. yedoense poukhanense* with *R. kaempferi*. Most Gable hybrids are hardy to −10° F or lower.

■ **GIRARD HYBRIDS:** Peter Girard Sr., a nurseryman from Geneva, Ohio, hybridized azaleas and rhododendrons for over 40 years. His evergreen azaleas are noted for their hardiness and compact growth. All are hardy to about −15° F.

■ **LINWOOD HYBRIDS:** These originated from the work of Dr. Charles Fischer, who developed hardy greenhouse-forcing azaleas in Linwood, New Jersey, in 1950. Later hybridizers carried on the work, producing cold-hardy landscape azaleas. The parents include Kurume and Kaempferi hybrids. More than 25 Linwood hybrids have been introduced. Most are hardy to between 0° and −5° F and have a low to medium growth habit.

■ **SHAMMARELLO HYBRIDS:** Tony Shammarello introduced evergreen azaleas noted for both cold hardiness and good growth habit. All are suitable for general landscape use and are hardy to −15° F.

■ **GLENN DALE HYBRIDS:** The Glenn Dale azaleas are the results of the largest breeding program in the United States. The hybrids range from early- to late-flowering plants and come in a wide variety of colors. Over 450 cultivars are named. Some cultivars are hardy to −10° F, but most are hardy to −5° F.

■ **BACK ACRES HYBRIDS:** B. Y. Morrison developed the Back Acres hybrids, which are noted for heat tolerance and large, substantial flowers. Generally, they bloom in midseason. These medium-size plants are cold-hardy to −5° F, but the flower buds are not as cold-resistant as those of the Glenn Dale hybrids.

■ **ROBIN HILL HYBRIDS:** The Robin Hill hybrids are very similar to the Satsuki and Kurume azaleas. They are late bloomers, averaging between 3 and 5 feet in height, with blooms in a variety of colors and flower types. The growth rate varies from slow to medium. Flowers range from single to hose-in-hose to full-double and may be in shades of white, pink, purple, and red. There are 69 named cultivars.

*'Girard's Crimson' not only offers bold color but also cold hardiness.*

*Joseph B. Gable introduced some of the first hardy evergreen azaleas in the United States. His 'Purple Splendor' blends beautifully in front of a 'Naomi Nautilus' rhododendron.*

## AZALEAS
*continued*

*Fall-blooming Encore azaleas are hybrids bred to bloom in a season other than spring. The blossoms of this 'Autumn Embers' complements the fall color of the leaves on the tree they surround.*

■ **SATSUKI HYBRIDS:** Satsuki azaleas are excellent landscape plants noted for their late flowers. Some have a spreading, low-growing habit, making them popular as bonsai plants; others attain medium height in 10 to 15 years. The plants are mostly rounded with a twiggy, compact growth; a few are pendulous. They are hardy to about –5° F. Because the flowers are late, the plants need protection from afternoon sun.

■ **PERICAT HYBRIDS:** Developed by Alphonse Pericat for greenhouse forcing, these hybrids are hardy outdoors in many areas. Most of the Pericats are as hardy as Kurume azaleas.

■ **NORTH TISBURY HYBRIDS:** Excellent as ground covers, trailing over walls, and in hanging baskets, North Tisbury hybrids are dwarf, spreading plants propagated by Polly Hill of Martha's Vineyard, Massachusetts.

■ **BELTSVILLE DWARFS:** These slow-growing plants are ideal for small gardens, borders, containers, and bonsai. They flower in early

spring but can be easily forced for late-winter bloom. Many Beltsville hybrids are true genetic dwarfs. Plants are hardy to –10° F.

■ **GREENWOOD HYBRIDS:** Greenwoods are a new group of evergreen azaleas for the Northwest. These hybrids range from low to medium in height and overall size. The Greenwood hybrids are hardy to –10° F and are well-suited for the East and the West.

■ **AUGUST KEHR HYBRIDS:** August Kehr is not a large hybrid group, but the few hybrids that exist produce excellent double-flowering plants. They are hardy to –5° F.

■ **HARRIS HYBRIDS:** These hybrids are just becoming known throughout the country. Over 30 plants have been introduced. Nearly all are hardy to –5° F.

■ **SCHROEDER HYBRIDS:** Developed in the 1970s for cold hardiness by Dr. Henry Schroeder, this group is also known for its attractive foliage and compact growth habit. All are hardy to about –15° F.

■ **ENCORE HYBRIDS:** The newest group of evergreen azaleas, Encore hybrids, were the dream of Robert E. Lee, who wanted to repeat the spring beauty of azaleas by manipulating them to bloom at other times of the year. In crossing spring-flowering azaleas with a rare summer-blooming azalea, he produced a group of hybrids that bloom over an extended period of time. The genetic diversity of the Encore hybrids results in a wide range of plant sizes and flower colors. All bloom in both spring and fall. Some bloom sporadically all summer long.

## DECIDUOUS AZALEAS

Native to North America, China, Europe, Japan, and Korea, deciduous azalea species number approximately 36. They include some of the most common garden azalea species.

Typically, deciduous azaleas have large flowers in white, yellow, pink, orange, or red. Most produce thin leaves in early spring just after the plants finish blooming, sometimes while they are in flower. Later-flowering species bloom after the plants leaf out. In fall, deciduous azaleas turn an attractive yellow, red, or purple.

Deciduous azaleas are prone to powdery mildew. Selecting mildew-resistant varieties or spraying plants with fungicides keeps plants attractive all summer and ensures a bright show of fall color. Most deciduous azaleas tolerate cold and are well-adapted to growing in warm regions.

The parent species of deciduous azalea hybrids were introduced to Western Europe and England from the late 1600s to the early 1800s. Developed in Belgium, the Ghent and Mollis hybrids were the descendants of these

early plant introductions. Today, Mollis and Ghent hybrids have generally been replaced by newer cultivars.

The first improved deciduous azalea hybrids were developed in the 1870s. Anthony Waterer and his son crossed the Ghents with the Chinese azalea and other species. They named the resulting hybrids after their nursery, Knap Hill.

Recent introductions of deciduous azaleas include the Windsor hybrids, selected from seedlings by Sir Eric Savill in the Savill Gardens, Windsor Great Park, England.

In the early 1980s, the University of Minnesota released the Northern Lights series. These deciduous hybrids are very hardy—to at least –35° F—and perform well in more moderate climates.

## AZALEA BLOSSOMS

Azaleas can often be distinguished by flower color. For example, you can find deciduous azalea blossoms in shades of yellow, orange, white, pink, and red. A few have purple blossoms. Evergreen azalea flowers, on the other hand, have white, red, pink, or purple blooms; some approach a red-orange. There are no yellow-flowered or deep-blue-flowered evergreen azaleas.

The bloom period for evergreen and deciduous azaleas differs according to geographic location. In tropical areas, azaleas bloom sporadically year-round. The farther north azaleas are planted, the shorter the blooming period. However, the bloom is heavier and the display is better. Farther south, the period is extended but the display is scattered and less decorative.

In central Florida, azaleas start blooming in fall (October) and continue into March. The flowering period in the San Francisco area ranges from mid-September to May, starting with Belgian and Glenn Dale hybrids and ending with Kaempferi and Satsuki azaleas. In the Southeast, Belgian hybrids and Glenn Dales start blooming in August and continue all winter. In Washington, D.C., and Seattle, the flowering period for azaleas extends from mid-April to July.

## AZALEA GROWING RANGE

The conditions in many parts of North America are ideal for growing azaleas. Many cultivars, especially the Southern Indian hybrids, do well in the South; others such as Kaempferi hybrids and deciduous azaleas are sufficiently hardy to perform well in Maine. Deciduous azaleas do well over most of the United States. Evergreen azaleas grow especially well on the East Coast of the

*This deciduous azalea from the Northern Light series is cold-hardy to –35° F.*

United States because the climate is similar to that of their native Japan. In Canada, few evergreen azaleas survive, but some deciduous azaleas are quite cold-hardy and will survive the Canadian winter. Rhododendrons can be found in Canada, especially with the introduction of new hybrids hardy to Zone 4.

### EVERGREEN AZALEA BLOOM PERIOD

| Area of Country | Period of Bloom |
| --- | --- |
| Central Florida | October to March |
| San Francisco | September to May |
| Southeastern United States | August through spring |
| Washington, D.C. | Mid-April to July |
| Seattle | Mid-April to July |

# RHODODENDRONS

Rhododendrons are best known for their dramatic, colorful flowers, but they are also valuable as landscape plants. From compact, sun-loving shrubs perfect for the rock garden to small understory trees, rhododendrons are available in a tremendous variety of sizes and shapes.

Though the enthusiast need not understand the complexities of rhododendron taxonomy, it helps to understand that rhododendrons are divided into three groups: elepidotes, lepidotes, and vireyas. There are broad differences among these groups in physical characteristics, flowering season, flower size and shape, and foliage.

*Typical of the elepidotes, 'Cynthia' is a robust grower with large, thick leaves and large flower trusses.*

## RHODODENDRON GROUPS

**ELEPIDOTE:** Elepidote means without scales. The term applies to rhododendrons that are evergreen, have broad leaves (broader than lepidotes), and no scales on the undersides of their leaves.

These rhododendrons bloom for an extended period. You can easily recognize them as rhododendrons by the robust appearance of their large, thick, dark leaves, stocky stems, and large flower trusses. As a group, elepidotes grow faster and larger than most azaleas and lepidote rhododendrons.

Elepidote rhododendrons grow best along both coasts of the United States, where summer and winter temperatures are not extreme (Zones 5 through 8). Summer heat probably kills more plants than winter cold. Although low temperatures will freeze flower buds, they seldom kill plants that are adapted to the region. Heat, on the other hand, can stress plants severely, and over time it results in death.

Many new rhododendron hybrids and improved species continue to enter the market as the quest for better plants continues. Breeders have been able to improve sun tolerance, cold hardiness, and disease and insect resistance in elepidote rhododendrons, and they have developed plants with more compact habits. They continue to work to develop a yellow-flowered elepidote rhododendron that blooms reliably after temperatures drop below –5° to –10° F. They are also trying to develop rhododendrons with true-blue flowers and other varieties with deep, pure-red flowers and good plant habit, cold hardiness, and ease of culture.

**LEPIDOTE:** Lepidote means scaly. On the underside of the leaf of a lepidote rhododendron are small scales, which resemble dots to the naked eye (see page 9). Lepidote rhododendrons have small leaves, usually less than 4 inches long; most small-leaf rhododendrons are lepidotes.

Although only a few lepidote hybrids existed a century ago, they have become more numerous and are valuable garden plants. Many are hardier than elepidote hybrids and offer an interesting change of foliage color from summer to winter.

*Like other lepidotes, 'Aglo' has small, dark green leaves and bears flowers in small trusses. It is hardy to –15° F and sun-tolerant.*

*This 'Dawn Chorus' shows the open habit of both plant and flowers typical of the vireyas. Note the shiny, dark green leaves and relaxed flower trusses.*

Because lepidote hybrids resemble azaleas in leaf size, they are often confused with azaleas. But compared with azaleas, their leaves are darker green and thicker with blunt ends. Flowers are borne in small trusses rather than as individual blossoms. Many are much more cold-hardy than azaleas and can withstand temperatures as low as –25° F. Lepidotes are also more difficult to propagate than evergreen azaleas, making it important to distinguish one from the other so as to use the correct rooting hormones.

The flowering period for both elepidote and lepidote rhododendrons is long; however, each individual plant blooms only once a year. Early bloomers hold flowers for as long as a month when the temperature is cool. Because plant activity increases as temperatures rise, plants that flower during warm weather may have blooms lasting only a week or two.

## RHODODENDRON SPECIES

In addition to the many available hybrid rhododendrons, many species rhododendrons are suitable for the home gardener. These rhododendron species range from small dwarf varieties to trees over 80 feet high, with foliage and flowers of great diversity. Several of these species are native to North America. The interest in rhododendron species is increasing with the interest in native plants.

## VIREYA RHODODENDRONS

The vireya group of rhododendrons is made up of approximately 300 species. The flowers of this group are firm, appearing almost waxed or artificial. Vireya rhododendrons, often called Malaysian rhododendrons, are tropical species and hybrids of rhododendrons native mostly to New Guinea. They grow year-round in their native habitat and therefore do not have a strong seasonal rhythm affected by day length or temperature. Some of the vireya species are epiphytes, which means they can grow in the air. Because of this, vireyas require excellent drainage, even more so than other rhododendrons.

Several features easily distinguish vireyas from other rhododendrons and azaleas. Their plant habit is generally more open than the habit of other rhododendrons, and their trusses are more lax. Scales cover their leaves, stems, and in some cases flowers. Leaves are shiny on the upper surface and grow in whorls around the stem. Also, they are often thick, tough, and not easily torn or damaged.

Individual flowers are often more tubular than those of azaleas or other rhododendrons. Flower colors include white, cream, orange, yellow, salmon, pink, and red. Vireyas can bloom more than once a year; they do not flower in any particular season. Some cultivars bloom almost continuously if plants are healthy. Vireyas produce long-tailed seeds.

Despite the large number of species, vireyas have remained largely unused as ornamental plants until recently. They are becoming increasingly popular as house- or greenhouse plants in the North and as outside plants in frost-free regions such as Southern California. They adapt easily to pot culture if the potting medium is light and porous, similar to the organic matter in which they grow in the wild. A mix of 1 part sphagnum peat moss and 3 parts pine bark will do. Indoors, vireyas need good light and a well-drained acid potting mix made up of 1 part pine bark (¼-inch size), 1 part peat moss, and 1 part perlite. Vireyas growing in containers respond well to frequent pruning and light fertilization.

*The elepidote rhododendron 'Ingrid Mehlquist', a yakushimanum hybrid, grows into a dense, compact plant with tight flower trusses.*

# CAMELLIAS

Although camellias resemble rhododendrons in some respects—their leaf shapes, branch configurations, and cultural needs—they are not closely related. Camellias belong to a distinctly different family of plants, the family *Theaceae*, of which the tea plant (*Camellia sinensis*) is commercially important.

The home of the camellia is China and lands bordering China to the east, west, and south, including parts of India, Burma, Korea, Formosa, and Japan. The native habitat is a picturesque world of gently sloping wooded hillsides and sparse forests. In misty valleys with damp, humus-rich soil, camellias grow into stately, moss-covered trees over 30 feet tall with smooth, gray trunks more than a foot thick.

To the ancient Chinese, camellias produced the ideal blossoms: smooth, flat petals; rounded form; perfect symmetry; and a conspicuous ring of golden stamens clustered at the center. The revered camellia was a favorite flower to paint, cup in the hands to ponder blemish-free beauty, float on the surface of water, and adorn the secret gardens of the emperors. Some camellia trees were so sacred to the ancient Chinese that it was forbidden to take a cutting or even to gather seeds.

In the wild, camellias are successful understory plants, finding good company among tall oaks and other durable deciduous trees. In forest clearings, they form "forests within a forest." Indeed, Descanso Gardens, just north of Los Angeles, presents a realistic replica of a primeval forest. Occupying many acres on the slopes of a canyon, this magnificent camellia forest is threaded with trails and shaded by majestic California live oaks.

## CAMELLIA HISTORY

The first interest in camellias as a source of tea was in China. Ancient lore suggests that it was quite by accident that a Chinese emperor discovered tea when leaves from an overstory plant fell into a pot of boiling water. The resulting aroma and flavor introduced tea as a new beverage.

For centuries, the Chinese used oil extracted from the seeds of tea plants as cooking oil and hair oil. It was not until later that they appreciated the beauty of the flowers or selected them for their ornamental value. Temple priests in China were the first to appreciate the beauty of camellias. The Buddhist love of natural beauty resulted in the selection and propagation of superior ornamental plants.

Japan has two highly ornamental native species, *C. japonica* and *C. sasanqua*, which were put to use in breeders' efforts to develop ornamental plants for gardens.

Although the first ornamental camellias arrived in the United States in 1798 in the form of *C. japonica*, it was not until the 1940s that interest in camellias increased. Throughout the 19th century, plant explorers brought camellias to the warmer West Coast and Deep South, where large collections were amassed from the 1830s until the present time. Recently hybridized hardier forms now allow gardeners over a much wider geographic range to enjoy the beauty of camellias.

## LANDSCAPE VALUE

Even if camellias never bloomed, their lovely evergreen foliage would make them worthy of any garden. The leaves are oval, pointed, and slightly toothed along the edges. Beautiful and sensual, they are deep green on the top

**Camellias are outstanding understory plants in their native habitat, such as this open woodland setting.**

*Single flowers, 'Yuletide'*

*Anemone-form blooms, 'Winter's Fire'*

*Peony-form, 'Kramer's Supreme'*

*Semidouble, 'Tinsie' blossoms*

*Rose-form-double, 'Helen Bower'*

*Formal-double, 'Contessa Lavinia Maggi'*

and light green on the underside and have the glossy feel of polished leather.

The sinuous, gray branches of camellia plants are pliable and ideal for training against the side of a house as an espalier.

As camellia plants age, they tend to shed their lower branches, leaving a clump of sleek, upright main trunks with smooth, gray bark supporting a dense overhead canopy. In poor soils, the trunks can become distorted, twisting and writhing to form impenetrable thickets. The trunks and branches may support vigorous populations of green algae, lichens, and epiphytic plants such as Spanish moss, heightening their aura of mystery.

The lush, dark foliage is a perfect foil for the best feature of the camellia—its showy, solitary, rounded flowers. Blossoms range from pristine white to all shades of pink to the deepest of reds. Many are variegated. The American Camellia Society has developed six classifications for camellia flower forms: single, semidouble, anemone-form, peony-form, rose-form-double, and formal-double (see examples above). The society has also specified five size categories for the blossoms: miniature, which are up to 2½ inches wide; small, ranging from 2½ to 3 inches across; medium, 3 to 4 inches across; large, 4 to 5 inches across; and very large, which are wider than 5 inches.

Camellias usually bloom between September and April (later in cold areas). Bloom seasons are classified as early (early fall through December), midseason (January through mid-March), and late (late March and later). These flowering periods are variable. Unusually warm or cold weather conditions can affect a particular variety's bloom season by several weeks. Also, camellias planted in colder climates bloom later than those grown in warmer regions.

## ADAPTATION

Most camellias are sensitive to frost and freezing, which restricts their use as outdoor ornamental shrubs to the Southeast and the Pacific Coast. However, in cold climates, they can be grown indoors, especially in greenhouses or in sunrooms. Many miniature varieties have been developed as flowering houseplants. They grow well indoors, provided nighttime temperatures are about 45° F and the air is humid.

# TYPES OF CAMELLIAS

*A camellia used as an accent plant in the landscape bends under the weight of its flowers in April.*

Although their numbers are few in the United States, camellias offer tremendously diverse variety for warm-climate landscapes. The majority of the camellias on the market today are one of three species—japonica, sasanqua, or reticulata—or hybrids of one of these species.

## CAMELLIA JAPONICA

Japanese camellia (*Camellia japonica*) and its 5,000 cultivars are the best known and most popular of the camellias. Japonica—as it is commonly known—is a large shrub or small tree with glossy green leaves; it usually has an upright habit. Most mature varieties grow between 8 and 10 feet tall and do best in partial shade. Japonicas can endure occasional drops in temperature to near 0° F, and a few varieties are more cold-hardy, tolerating short periods of temperatures as low as –5° F.

## CAMELLIA SASANQUA

Sasanquas are the next most commonly grown camellias. Actually, varieties of three species—*Camellia sasanqua*, *C. hiemalis*, and *C. vernalis*—make up this group. As a rule, the sasanquas are large shrubs or small trees with glossy leaves. Their growth is bushier than that of japonicas, and their leaves are smaller. Sasanquas make excellent hedges and foundation and screen plantings. Some are also used as ground covers, espaliers, and container plants. The sasanquas are not as hardy as japonica varieties, and their flowers are not as showy. But they bloom profusely and are more sun-tolerant than japonicas.

## CAMELLIA RETICULATA

The third most popular group is made up of the reticulatas. From *C. reticulata*, they are small- to medium-size plants native to southern China. They have a more open and upright branching habit than japonicas or sasanquas. Leaves are large and matte rather than glossy. The flowers are quite large, 6 inches or more across, in colors ranging from light pink to red. Reticulatas are not as cold-hardy as other camellia species. Their lower limit is 25° F, but there is some variation in hardiness.

## HYBRID CAMELLIAS

Like hybrid rhododendrons, hybrid camellias are increasing the diversity and garden-worthiness of the three species. Camellia hybrids boast a wide array of colors and cold hardiness levels. Through hybridizing with the newly discovered yellow *C. chrysantha*, the color range is expanding with exciting new hues, such as peach, apricot, and orange. Work to increase fragrance, cold hardiness, and heat tolerance is continuing.

**HIGO HYBRIDS:** Among the oldest hybrids are the Higos. These are a group of japonica cultivars that were unknown to the Western world until the early 19th century because they grew mainly on the Japanese island of Kyushu and were not exported. Higo is the name of the district in which they were first developed.

Higos are hybrids of selected cultivars of *C. japonica* with *C. japonica rusticana*, a cold-hardy subspecies. In Japan, they are generally used as bonsai or container plants, but gardeners in the United States grow them in their landscapes.

Higo flowers are unique among camellias. Nearly all are singles with flat petals. Each flower has a multitude of stamens (100 to 200), which are arranged in a decorative, tight hemisphere in the center of the flower. Blooms vary from solid shades of white, pink, and red to patterns of blotches and stripes. Some of the cultivars have fragrant flowers.

**OTHER HYBRIDS:** After the introduction of *Camellia japonica* and its many cultivars, interest in the other camellia species slowly developed in England. In 1942, J. C. Williams made the first cross between two species: *C. saluenensis* and *C. japonica*. Subsequent hybrids of these two species are known as Williamsii hybrids. Today, breeding efforts continue in the United States, Australia, New Zealand, Japan, China, England, and Europe.

## ACKERMAN HYBRIDS: COLD-HARDY CAMELLIAS

Camellias can be grown successfully outdoors in the United States along the East Coast from Virginia to Florida, through the Gulf Coast to Texas, and from Southern California to coastal Oregon and Washington on the West Coast. Normally, these plants are too susceptible to cold injury to be grown farther north than hardiness Zone 8a.

Recently, however, breeders have introduced new camellia hybrids that are classified as winter-hardy, making the camellia no longer a perk only for gardeners in frost-free areas. Withstanding temperatures of –5° to –10° F, the new hybrids are certain to become popular in today's gardens. They should be given some winter protection from sun and wind for the first year after transplanting. Spring planting is recommended in all but hardiness Zone 8 and warmer areas.

The changes in hardiness of some camellia hybrids was brought about through the resiliency of the species *C. oleifera*. The relatively mild winters in the 1950s through the early 1970s encouraged many Eastern gardeners to plant camellias farther north than where they are normally hardy. But the winters of 1977 to 1979, when temperatures around Washington, D.C., fell to –10° F, brought the glory of camellias in this area to an end. The result was a drastic reduction in camellia culture in the mid-Atlantic area.

At the National Arboretum in Washington, D.C., 900 camellias were killed to the ground during those two cold winters. However, one *C. oleifera* plant

*This Ackerman hybrid, 'Winter's Waterlily', flowers in fall and is cold-hardy to –15° F, extending the camellia belt north into colder climates, at least to Zone 6.*

survived. It not only lived but flowered fully and continued to bloom each year afterward.

Dr. William Ackerman, a research horticulturist at the arboretum, decided that hybridizers needed this hardy seedling to develop a new cold-hardy group of camellias.

After years of crossing *C. oleifera* with plants that produce more landscape-worthy flowers, he introduced 20 new cultivars. Eighteen are cold-hardy in Zone 6. The hardiest are 'Winter's Rose', 'Winter's Beauty', and 'Winter's Waterlily', all of which survive temperatures down to –10° to –15° F.

# AZALEAS, RHODODENDRONS & CAMELLIAS IN THE LANDSCAPE

Their diversity in size, texture, and flower color means that azaleas, rhododendrons, and camellias can fit almost any landscape need. As woody evergreens, they make reliable permanent plantings and establish a garden's framework. They tolerate shade, have showy flowers, and display foliage that is as ornamental as the blooms. They are versatile plants that can anchor many desirable garden design features.

Much of the beauty of rhododendrons, azaleas, and camellias lies in how well they complement one another and the plantings around them. If you are replacing a few plants or planting a new garden, carefully consider the effect of each plant's growth habit, mature height, spread, and foliage density. Also consider foliage texture, flowering time, and color of nearby plants.

**HABIT:** Rhododendrons, azaleas, and camellias range from trees to open shrubs to sprawling ground covers. Some grow slowly and remain compact even at maturity; others become large in only a few years. The shrubs vary in their shapes, too. Some are upright and spreading; others are globose, or round.

**FLOWERING TIME:** Bloom periods for rhododendrons, azaleas, and camellias vary considerably. For example, most azaleas flower in spring, but the roseshell azalea blooms in midsummer. Most camellias bloom during winter through early summer, but sasanquas flower in fall. Flowering times also vary from year to year, depending on the weather. A warm spell will speed flowering; cooler weather will slow it down.

Consider flowering times for effective companion plantings. For example, pairing Spanish bluebells (*Hyacinthoides hispanica*) with red azaleas requires precise selection of varieties so they will reach peak bloom together. If you want several varieties of rhododendrons to bloom simultaneously, make your selections based on their bloom periods (see page 50 for guidelines). But be aware that flowering time will vary from year to year. No matter how well you plan, the same combination of plants may not bloom together.

**COLOR:** An obvious but essential element in planning a garden is color. Do the blooms of neighboring shrubs complement one another or do they clash? To avoid clashing colors, select varieties that bloom at different times.

Foliage color is important, too. How do the colors of the leaves of the plants you hope to combine look with one another? A plant with blue-gray leaves may not harmonize with one bearing yellow-green leaves. Foliage can

*Mature rhododendrons are valuable as landscape screens, in this case for privacy. The large rhododendron shown here also serves as a specimen plant and is showy against the dark green background. Its broad foliage contrasts effectively with the needled evergreen tree behind it.*

compete with flowers, too. For example, a planting of several strikingly variegated shrubs draws attention even when planted among stoplight-red azaleas.

## TIPS

Plant habits, flowering times, and colors are the main criteria for creating a beautiful and healthy garden with azaleas, rhododendrons, or camellias. The following tips will help you use them with finesse in your landscape.

■ Large cultivars of rhododendrons and camellias make striking specimen plants. One plant can become a focal point in the garden.

■ Tall rhododendrons go well with natural landscapes, such as woodlands, or planted on the far side of a pond.

■ Ground-hugging, dwarf azaleas are ideal for confined spaces.

■ When interplanted with other shrubs or perennials, rhododendrons, azaleas, and camellias become breathtaking accents, adding color to flower beds and borders.

■ Taller camellia cultivars have pliable branches that can be bent and secured to a wall or fence to create an espalier, in patterns ranging from parallel lines to fan shapes.

■ Rhododendrons, azaleas, and camellias look best when planted in groups.

## LANDSCAPE USES

Some plants are useful in only a few landscape situations. Not so with camellias, azaleas, and rhododendrons. There is a species or hybrid to make the right statement in any landscape—from containers to beds and borders, from bonsai to hedges, and from rock gardens to woodlands.

**BEDS AND BORDERS:** Beds are prepared gardens in open areas of the yard. They can be any size or shape. Because they are not backed by plants or structures, beds have good air circulation, which helps prevent powdery mildew. All sides of a bed are visible, so the tallest plants should be in the center. Take care to locate beds where they will be shaded from hot afternoon sun, which burns leaves and fades blossoms. Azaleas can tolerate an open, sunny bed better than rhododendrons and camellias.

Borders are garden areas at the perimeter of a yard. They may be backed by fences, trees, buildings, or hedges. Because they are viewed from the front only, place tall plants to the rear. Afternoon shade over the border protects plants and is especially beneficial for rhododendrons and camellias. Trees or buildings to the south or west of the border will shield plants from afternoon sun. Dark green evergreen trees or hedges backing the

border are an effective contrast to the flowers, magnifying their intensity in the landscape.

**WINDBREAKS:** Azaleas, rhododendrons, and camellias do not make good windbreaks. Strong winds are drying and cause leaf burn. But you can locate these plants on the lee side of a windbreak, where they dress up its plain facade beautifully.

**HEDGES:** Azaleas take heavy pruning, sending out new branches from anywhere along the stem, so they make beautiful sheared hedges. They may also be allowed to grow freely into informal hedges, which are not sheared. Camellias are best pruned into unsheared informal hedges, as are some of the lepidote rhododendrons.

**SCREENS:** Landscape screens establish privacy zones. Rhododendrons and camellias as well as some of the taller azaleas make good screening plants. Their lush foliage, height, and striking bloom create a beautiful shield. Provide afternoon shade for rhododendrons and camellias used as screens by planting taller evergreen trees, such as Norway spruce or Scotch pine, nearby. These trees also make an effective windbreak for the screens.

*Low-growing camellias are effective edging plants. They make a striking border and blend well with the broad-leaved foliage behind them.*

*Bright colors can be used to terminate a garden view. This yellow deciduous azalea draws the eye down the path to its end.*

# SPECIALTY LANDSCAPES

*With their color and shape, azaleas make a stunning addition to an oriental garden. Plants are pruned more formally here than if used in an open woodland setting.*

Azaleas, rhododendrons, and camellias adapt well to any landscape style. Should you have a specific garden style or particular container in mind, a well-chosen species or hybrid would certainly fit beautifully. Azaleas, rhododendrons, and camellias lend themselves particularly well to woodland plantings, oriental landscapes, rock gardens, and containers.

## WOODLAND PLANTINGS

It is in the woodland that azaleas, camellias, and rhododendrons reign supreme. Some of the finest woodland gardens in the world rely heavily on rhododendrons and azaleas for intense color. Camellias add color to southern gardens during the winter months.

A wonderful companion plant for woodland azaleas and for early-flowering rhododendrons is the white-flowering dogwood (*Cornus florida*), which blooms at the same time and contrasts effectively with the predominant pinks and reds of azaleas.

The ideal woodland environment is one in which deep-rooted, tall deciduous trees or tall, open-crown evergreens have had their lower branches trimmed away, allowing free air movement and creating dappled shade.

## ORIENTAL LANDSCAPES

Rhododendrons, camellias, and especially azaleas are ideal plants for Japanese- or Chinese-style gardens. *Rhododendron yakushimanum, R. kiusianum,* lepidote rhododendrons, and Satsuki azaleas are especially appropriate selections for an oriental-style garden.

In an oriental landscape, the plants are often severely pruned to attain a specific shape. Here, foliage color and shape are the desired goals; promoting flowering is less important. The sparse, pruned foliage of certain cultivars can be used as a delicate accent to the oriental landscape.

The following three oriental styles adapt easily to North American home landscapes.

**NATURAL:** In this style, plants are massed along a slope, next to a bridge or rustic building, or beside a lake to create a natural, untamed look.

**SHEARED:** Drastic shearing to give a shrub the shape of a dome or a pillow is the desired effect in this sort of oriental landscape. The smooth mounds introduce a soft, tranquil mood, as cushions of moss would do on a smaller scale.

Heavy shearing reduces the number of blossoms each year. To keep a smooth contour requires shearing the shrubs twice a year (in spring immediately after the blossoms fade and again in late June to early July). The second shearing removes any flower buds that have developed.

Although the second shearing offers azaleas little time to produce new flower buds, it actually creates an attractive effect. It encourages the emergence of rich green foliage against which the few blossoms that do develop are highlighted like stars.

Any late vegetative growth in fall will be above the flowering shoots and should be trimmed back to maintain the effect all year.

**ARTISTICALLY PRUNED:** To create this type of landscape effect, the thicket of lower main branches is thinned out dramatically and the lower side branches are stripped away. A dense canopy of foliage, like an umbrella or a mushroom, is allowed to form. This style of pruning emphasizes sinuous lines and creates the illusion of age and sculpturing by the elements—the kind of sculpturing that might happen over many years on an exposed cliff or a mountaintop.

## ROCK GARDENS

Because many species of azaleas and rhododendrons come from mountainous regions, a rock garden is an ideal place to display them. The rock garden can be located along a partially shaded slope backed by a windbreak of tall evergreens.

The most beautiful rock gardens combine three elements: plants, rocks, and water—especially water that trickles over the rocks and creates informal, natural-looking pools. Water is a desirable feature near azaleas and rhododendrons. It not only helps create a cool, humid environment, but also mirrors the flower display, doubling its color impact.

Most rock gardens featuring rhododendrons benefit from an underground watering system. Rhododendrons are adapted to high altitudes, where they are constantly shrouded in mist; if subjected to desert-dry conditions for any length of time, they wilt and die. Rock gardeners particularly favor azaleas and the dwarf alpine rhododendron species and hybrids because they are shorter and slower growing. They will do well planted among the rocks in deep pockets of leaf mold and soil.

## CONTAINERS

Many rhododendrons, azaleas, and camellias—especially slow-growing and dwarf varieties—are suited to life in containers, whether in tubs on a patio or terrace, hanging baskets, or bonsai trays. In areas with alkaline or problem soils, growing these plants in containers makes good sense because it is easier to prepare a suitable soil mix for a container than to amend outdoor soil to make it suitable for growing. Even with slow-growing and dwarf varieties, pinching and pruning may be necessary to maintain an attractive shape.

Just about any camellia can be grown in a large container, and many varieties have been developed especially for pot culture. Indeed, some are small and compact and can be grown as houseplants, as long as the humidity is high. 'Nuccio's Gem' (white) and 'Nuccio's Cameo' (pink) are compact forms of *Camellia sasanqua* that will grow indoors.

Certain varieties of azaleas are particularly effective as hanging baskets. Some of the Belgian and Satsuki hybrids—such as 'Flame Creeper' and 'Pink Cascade'—have a naturally spreading, pendulous habit that can make a beautiful basket without tedious training.

When left unpruned, rhododendrons are a valuable addition to a woodland setting. Here they frame a walkway in an informal woodland area.

Though camellias are difficult to cultivate in hanging baskets, some spreading and pendulous sasanqua varieties and hybrids such as 'Tiny Princess' can be successful.

## PERSONALIZING YOUR LANDSCAPE

Now that you've had a glimpse of the beauty and landscape possibilities of rhododendrons, azaleas, and camellias, read on to learn how to best use these plants in your garden. The next section is devoted to helping you plant and care for your rhododendrons, azaleas, and camellias; it includes information on identifying and treating pests and diseases. The last section, an encyclopedia with descriptions of the most important species, varieties, and cultivars, will provide you with a wide range of plant choices suitable for your taste and climate.

As container plants, rhododendrons and azaleas are ideal. They add a portable accent to a patio, an entrance, or other close-contact areas of the landscape.

# GROWING RHODODENDRONS, AZALEAS & CAMELLIAS

*Rhododendrons do especially well when the cultivar selected matches the site and its exposure. This sheltered north-side nook protects plants from wind and provides beneficial shade.*

Follow these four keys to success when growing azaleas, rhododendrons, and camellias. First, choose the proper cultivar, one with a genetic makeup that can survive in your location. Second, select a spot in your garden that has the proper environment to grow it in. Third, plant properly. This is especially important for container-grown plants with roots confined to a small amount of soilless mix. Finally, monitor the plant's condition for its first three to four years, and maintain the plant with proper watering. Here are the specifics.

## PLANT SELECTION

With the right growing conditions, camellias, rhododendrons, and azaleas mature into healthy, attractive plants that bloom year after year. Once they become established, they should need little maintenance. But if a cultivar is not adapted to your garden, it will always require extra effort on your part to survive. Thus, your first and most important task when growing camellias, azaleas, and rhododendrons is to select plants that will thrive in your yard. Buying a plant just because it is offered for sale at a nearby nursery is no guarantee it will thrive. Instead, a good starting point for finding good cultivars is to ask local azalea, camellia, or rhododendron society members for advice.

## CLIMATE FIRST

No amount of cultural savvy can overcome a poor match between the plants and the site. The first step, then, is to become familiar with the growing conditions in your yard. Such factors as high and low temperatures, rainfall patterns, wind velocity, frost pockets, soil type, pH, drainage, sun intensity, and shade affect how plants grow; they're often the deciding factors when it comes to survival.

**COLD:** Cold hardiness is the most important factor when selecting azaleas, rhododendrons, and camellias. Generally, hybrids from species native to higher elevations do best in cool climates; those from tropical areas withstand more heat. However, some tropical species are from mountainous areas and don't tolerate heat. Azaleas, rhododendrons, and camellias flourish in many areas of North America, growing extremely well in areas close to an ocean or other large bodies of water, such as the Great Lakes.

Rhododendrons are adapted to a wide range of temperatures. Some cultivars withstand −35° F, whereas others don't tolerate temperatures below 40° F.

Azaleas do well over much of the United States, but they, too, vary in hardiness. The Southern Indian azaleas are not reliably cold-hardy north of Zone 7 on the East and West Coasts; some Gable, Shammarello, Girard, and Schroeder cultivars can withstand temperatures as low as −15° F. Deciduous azaleas are much hardier.

Camellias do best in areas where winter temperatures don't fall below 5° F. Of the most widely grown camellias, japonicas are the most cold-hardy; sasanquas are next, and reticulatas are the least hardy. Many camellias require little more than to be kept from freezing; they can grow under glass with little added heat. New Ackerman hybrids perform well at temperatures to −10° F, and some survive to −15° F.

**HEAT:** Heat tolerance is also a factor in plant selection; it becomes increasingly important in areas warmer than Zone 6. Most azaleas and rhododendrons cannot survive long periods of intense heat. Except for vireyas,

azaleas and camellias do better than rhododendrons in the Deep South. In areas such as Southern California and the lower South, heat-tolerant azalea hybrids, such as the Belgian Indians, yield better results.

*Select intermediate-size azaleas to use as transition plants. Here they blend high-growing shrubs and trees with lower-growing perennials.*

## MATCH SIZE TO SPACE

You should also consider the height and shape of mature plants when making your selection. Some azaleas and rhododendrons are low and compact; others are tall and loose. Camellias are more treelike and grow indefinitely. By matching the plants to the size of the space available for them, you won't have to relocate plants in a few years.

## NARROWING YOUR SELECTIONS

Once you know the conditions in your yard, you can select azaleas, rhododendrons, and camellias to match. All three species and their cultivars exhibit great genetic diversity in size, shape, flower color, and adaptability. The encyclopedia, which begins on page 48, can help you find the ones right for your yard.

To quickly pinpoint which azaleas, camellias, or rhododendrons thrive in your climate, check the adaptation maps on page 49. Each entry refers to one of those maps.

For more detailed information, contact the chapter of the azalea, camellia, or rhododendron society in your area, or visit the national associations' websites.

*In severe climates, you don't have to give up beauty for cold hardiness. This is 'Nova Zembla', an elepidote hardy to −25° F with tight trusses of red flowers.*

*To grow rhododendrons in a garden, look for a compact variety like this 'Bruce Brechtbill'.*

# SELECTING THE SITE

*This site, with the dapple shade and windbreak provided by tall trees, is ideal for rhododendrons.*

Azaleas, rhododendrons, and camellias evolved in areas of humus-rich, well-drained, acid soils, generally in mountainous areas with cool nights, high humidity, and plentiful summer rainfall. Many species evolved on the edges of woodlands or as understory plants, where they grew in shade for a portion of each day. If these conditions are not present naturally in your landscape, modify your yard to create this environment.

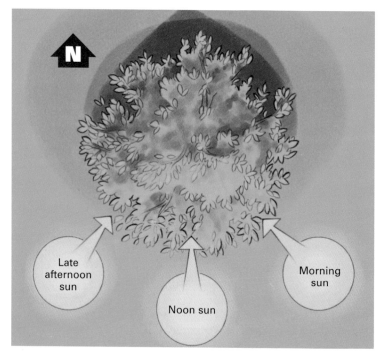

*Camellias, azaleas, and rhododendrons thrive in filtered shade (the medium-gray area). Before planting, pay attention to sun patterns to find the right spot for your shrubs.*

Late afternoon sun

Noon sun

Morning sun

## SHADING PLANTS

Shade is vital to rhododendrons, azaleas, and camellias. It affects almost every visible aspect of the plant, including the color of the foliage, compactness or legginess of the growth, cold hardiness, and abundance or lack of blooms. In general, all three plants grow best in the filtered shade of high tree branches, an environment similar to their native canopied habitats.

The amount of shade necessary for your rhododendrons, azaleas, and camellias depends on the cultivar and the region where it is growing. In areas where moisture is abundant (receiving at least 40 inches a year) and nights are cool (below 70° F), it's not critical that the plants receive only shade, unless the cultivar is sun-sensitive. But where summer droughts are common—which encompasses most areas of the country—an open, sunny location could be lethal.

However, even though it sounds contradictory, you should plant azaleas, rhododendrons, and camellias where they will receive as much sun as they can tolerate. When they grow in too little light, these plants become spindly and may not form flower buds. A site receiving moderate afternoon shade, such as beneath tall trees with high limbs or along the east or north side of a building, is appropriate; densely wooded areas are not.

Azaleas tolerate a greater light intensity than camellias or rhododendrons, but a lightly shaded area is best in all cases. In light shade, azaleas are less susceptible to dehydration, and flowers retain color and last longer. Afternoon shade will extend the bloom period for azaleas growing in warm areas.

Although most camellias prefer light shade, sasanqua cultivars usually can tolerate more sun than other camellias, especially in hot, dry climates. Where the humidity is high, such as the Pacific Northwest, all camellias can tolerate more sun than they can when growing in hot, dry climates. However, even in humid climates, white and pale pink blossoms may burn if exposed to sun. Only the darker colors do well in direct sun. Choose a site for camellias away from highly reflective walls or white fences, unless these surfaces are shaded or are along the north side of a building.

Should your yard be too shady, you may need to do some pruning to grow azaleas, camellias, and rhododendrons. If dense shade is cast by low-limbed evergreen or deciduous trees, you can increase the light reaching the shrubs by removing the lowest limbs of the trees. If the shade in your yard is produced by neighboring structures, such as walls of buildings, you can paint the walls a light color to reflect any available light onto the plants.

The shade of a tall tree is an ideal site for this rhododendron and its shade-loving companion plants— hosta, oxalis, epimedium, and ferns— which serve to gently blend the rhododendron into the surrounding lawn area.

## WINDBREAKS

In their native habitats, rhododendrons and azaleas are often found in protected areas, so they have not grown to endure strong winds. Plants dehydrate faster in sun and wind than in a still, shady environment. If roots are in frozen soil when the wind blows, the increased rate of dehydration can result in tissue damage and even death, because moisture is pulled out of the plant faster than the roots can replace it, especially if the temperature also rises.

Reducing the wind speed in your garden by planting a windbreak allows the plants to retain moisture and protects leaves from damage. A windbreak may be a wooden fence, a row of evergreen trees, or a hedge. Be aware that stagnant air can also be harmful to these plants, so the windbreak should not be so dense that it stops airflow.

Rhododendrons and camellias need more protection from wind than azaleas do, but azaleas also benefit from a windbreak. Shelter from wind and sun provided by windbreaks is especially important when plants are being grown at the extreme limits of their hardiness range.

Strong winds are most dangerous in extreme heat or cold, when the plants dry out quickly. For example, a plant that is recommended for Maine or Canada and is cold-hardy to –25° F could easily be severely damaged in an exposed site at a much warmer temperature.

In cold areas, it is important to protect camellias, azaleas, and rhododendrons on their south sides. The warmth of bright winter sun can cause stem tissue to expand. Then at night, when the temperature drops again, ice crystals form in the expanded cells, injuring the plant.

Windbreaks are effective for a distance of six to seven times their height, so a 7-foot-high hedge will slow wind velocity for a distance of 40 to 50 feet. Rhododendrons, azaleas, and camellias can be grown within that 40- to 50-foot no-wind zone. Solid walls and wooden fences alone are not always adequate, because wind hitting a solid barrier with great force can jump over it with equal velocity. A row of trees or shrubs absorbs the wind and allows some air through, weakening the force.

## FROST POCKETS

Avoid planting azaleas, rhododendrons, and camellias in frost pockets. These develop at the bases of slopes. Because cold air is dense, it slides to the bottom of the slope, so this area is colder than the top. Unless the base of the slope has good air circulation, which can help mix warm air with the cold, it is best to plant higher up on the slope than at the bottom.

# PREPARING THE SITE

*The easiest way to work in pine bark, sphagnum peat moss, or other amendments is with a rototiller.*

The first step in creating a healthy environment for azaleas, camellias, and rhododendrons is to plant them in the best possible soil. All three plants prefer a light, well-drained, acidic soil. Understanding the plants' soil needs and adjusting the soil to fit those needs will help ensure success.

## DETERMINING WHAT YOU HAVE

To find out whether your soil is conducive to the growth and health of rhododendrons, camellias, and azaleas, have it tested. County extension offices and private laboratories do the tests and provide accurate results plus recommendations for making changes. Contact these facilities for details on how to submit soil samples. In the meantime, here are a couple of tests you can do at home.

■ **CHECKING PH:** The preferred pH (acidity or alkalinity) for azaleas and rhododendrons is between 5 and 6. Camellias do best with soil pH levels between 6 and 6.5. Home soil-test kits help you determine whether your soil's pH is in that range. The kits give approximate, but useful, pH readings.

With some tests, you press strips of paper against wet soil; for others, you place a sample of soil in a special liquid. In most cases, pH is read by comparing the color change against a chart.

■ **TESTING FOR SOIL TYPE:** Azaleas, rhododendrons, and camellias prefer a rich, loamy-textured soil, which is composed of a balanced proportion of organic matter, clay,

and sand. The following tests will give you a rough idea of the type of soil in your yard.

■ **JAR TEST:** Take several teaspoon-size soil samples from the top 6 inches of your garden. Let the samples dry thoroughly, then pulverize them with a rolling pin. Next, fill a quart jar two-thirds full of water, stir in 1 teaspoon of dishwasher detergent, add the soil, cover, and shake vigorously.

Within a few minutes, sand particles will settle to the bottom of the jar. With a grease pencil, mark their level on the side of the jar. After two hours, the silt and organic matter will settle on top of the sand. Mark their levels. Finally, let the jar sit for several days to several weeks, however long it takes for the clay to settle out and the water to clear. Mark the top of the clay level. Now you can estimate the relative amount of the different components in your soil. If one type is more than one-half the total amount, that is the dominant soil type.

■ **RIBBON TEST:** The ribbon test is easier to do, but it is less precise than the jar test. Moisten a handful of soil, then roll it between your open palms to form a "snake." If the soil feels gritty and refuses to hold a shape, it's mostly sand. If it forms a 1- to 2-inch ribbon before falling apart, the soil is loamy. If the ribbon feels gritty, the soil is a sandy loam; if it's silky, it is a silty loam. The longer the ribbon, the more clay it contains. If you can form a long ribbon that is sticky, your soil is mostly clay.

■ **DRAINAGE:** Azaleas, rhododendrons, and camellias require moist soil for the best growth, but they don't do well sitting in water. If you are unsure how well your soil drains, dig a hole about a foot deep and fill it with water. Let it drain, then fill it again. The water should drain

## LOWERING SOIL PH

To acidify soil, apply iron sulfate. All amounts listed below are for 100 square feet of bed.

| pH Change | Iron Sulfate |
|-----------|--------------|
| 7.0 to 5.5 | 18.1 lbs. |
| 6.5 to 5.5 | 16.5 lbs. |
| 6.0 to 5.5 | 7.1 lbs. |

**Note:** *You can use sulfur to produce the same result. Apply 20 percent of the rate listed for iron sulfate. (Sulfur alone does not work if soil pH is above 7.)*
**Caution:** *Around living plants, apply no more than 1 pound per 100 square feet at a time to prevent root injury. This will lower soil pH approximately 0.2 of a pH unit.*

out. If it stays at the same level for several hours, the soil is poorly drained.

## MAKING IMPROVEMENTS

In less than ideal situations, you can improve the drainage, pH, and texture of your soil quite easily, making a suitable soil environment for azaleas, rhododendrons, and camellias. Simply amending the soil with organic matter will improve things, but when drainage is poor, you may need to raise the planting area.

Adding organic matter lightens heavy clay, improves drainage and aeration, and increases the moisture-holding capacity of sandy soil. It also provides an environment conducive to the presence of beneficial soil microbes, which help control root rot diseases and make mineral nutrients more readily available to plants, resulting in better plant health and insect and disease resistance. To amend soil, cover the planting area with 4 inches of organic matter, then dig the bed to a depth of 8 to 10 inches, thoroughly mixing the organic material with the topsoil.

The best organic material should have a long life in the soil, such as a mix of 75 percent fine pine bark and 25 percent coarse sphagnum peat moss. The resulting amended soil will be approximately 50 percent organic matter and will have a spongy feel when you squeeze it. Other suitable materials include composted redwood, pine, or fir bark.

If the bed needs raising, add topsoil and organic matter to bring the bed 12 to 18 inches above the existing soil level.

The area to be amended and raised should ideally be 4 feet in diameter for a single plant. In the case of multiple plants, the entire bed should be amended and raised. The bed can be smaller if there isn't enough room, but the amended area should be as large as possible.

■ **PH ADJUSTMENTS:** You can temporarily lower pH by digging sphagnum peat moss into the bed before planting. But a more accurate, long-term way to reduce pH is to add a soil acidifier such as iron (or ferrous) sulfate or sulfur as you prepare the planting bed. See Lowering Soil pH on page 28 for amounts to use. Mix the full amount of iron sulfate into the topsoil and till it in. Make sure to water the soil several times with a hose to wash away excess salts before planting. Iron sulfate is a salt, and, like table salt, it will kill roots and burn foliage if applied in excess.

To gradually lower the pH around established plants, spread iron sulfate on top of the soil from 6 inches around the trunk to 1½ feet outside the drip line, being careful

This soil has a good, crumbly texture, which allows it to drain well and have adequate aeration.

not to use more than 1 pound per 100 square feet at a time. On younger plants with smaller root systems, spread it only a few inches outside the drip line. If necessary, repeat applications (not more than once a month). Follow each application with 1 inch of water to flush the chemical through the soil. Fertilizing with ammonium sulfate or other acid-forming fertilizers helps maintain the lowered pH.

The jar test shows the results of soil settling out in layers of sand, silt, clay, and organic matter. This sample shows about 2 inches of sand, ½ inch of silt and ½ inch of clay.

If the soil pH is too acidic, use limestone to raise it. See amounts to use in Raising Soil pH, below.

## RAISING SOIL PH

To raise pH, use ground limestone. The amounts listed below will raise the pH by one unit. All amounts are for 100 square feet.

| Soil | Limestone |
|------|-----------|
| Loam | 7–8 lbs. |
| Clay | 9–10 lbs. |
| Sandy | 6 lbs. |

**Caution:** *To avoid calcium toxicity, do not apply more than 7 pounds of limestone per 100 square feet at a time.*

# PLANTING

Loosen the roots of container-grown plants so they'll grow into the native soil. Or cut slits in the root ball (right) to stop roots from growing in circles.

Field-grown plants have heavier root balls and should be handled by the ball, not the stem, to prevent ripping the roots off the stem.

Lay a tool handle or straight stick over the planting hole to check the depth of the root ball, which should be about 1 inch above the soil surface.

Lift loosened roots and place soil under them so they extend into the soil surrounding the root ball.

Pack soil firmly around the roots with hands, not feet. Too much pressure on the roots damages them or tears them from the stem.

Once you have found the perfect location for azaleas, rhododendrons, and camellias, and have tested and amended your soil, it is time to buy the plants and get them in the ground.

## TIMING

The best time to buy and plant azaleas and rhododendrons is early fall in Zone 6 and warmer areas and in early spring elsewhere. Fall planting is best because the shrubs are not actively growing or flowering at this time. Both of these processes demand extra moisture from a root system that is not yet established in the soil. Camellias transplant best in spring.

In areas where the soil freezes early in fall and deeply over winter—hardiness Zone 5 and colder—it is better to plant azaleas and rhododendrons in early spring so the root system has time to become established. Applying mulch at planting will prevent the soil from freezing early or deeply over winter, so fall-planted shrubs will continue to develop new roots late into the year.

Check plants carefully before buying them. They should be old enough to have reached flowering size. Most rhododendrons, azaleas, and camellias sold at nurseries have reached that stage of maturity and are ready for planting in the landscape. Also, check the foliage. It should be deep green; yellow or burned edges indicate improper watering. Plants should also be insect- and disease-free and have a moist root ball.

## PLANTING

Plant rhododendrons, azaleas, and camellias immediately after purchase if possible. If there is any delay between purchase and planting, provide shade and a daily watering.

The planting method you use depends on whether your shrub was grown in a container or in the ground. No matter which production method the nursery used, start by digging a hole 4 feet in diameter and 1 inch shallower than the depth of the root ball for each shrub. The root ball must sit on solid ground, and it should extend about 1 inch above the existing soil level. This keeps the shrub's roots at the correct depth. More rhododendrons, azaleas, and camellias die from being planted too deep than from any other cause except improper watering.

Place the root ball on the undisturbed soil in the bottom of the hole. If you dug too deep and disturbed the soil in the bottom of the hole, tamp it down before setting the root ball. Soil that is not tamped will settle when watered so that the root ball will sink. To

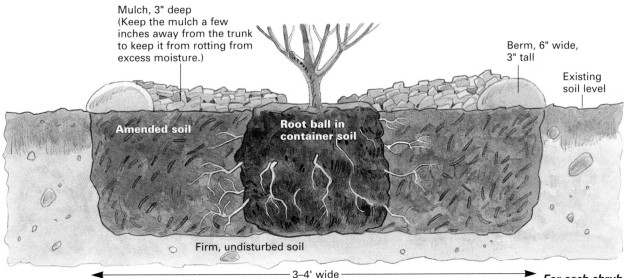

Mulch, 3" deep
(Keep the mulch a few
inches away from the trunk
to keep it from rotting from
excess moisture.)

Berm, 6" wide,
3" tall

Existing
soil level

Amended soil

Root ball in
container soil

Firm, undisturbed soil

3–4' wide

check the level of the root ball, lay a straight stick or tool handle across the top of the hole.

## SPECIAL HANDLING

**CONTAINER-GROWN PLANTS:** Container-grown shrubs require more attention at planting than do field-grown plants. The soilless mixes in which they are potted are different from the soil in your garden, so roots refuse to grow out of the container mix into the garden soil, and moisture does not move from the native soil to the container soil. Thus, the soilless root ball can dry out quickly, killing the plant. To solve this problem, tease the roots from the root ball so that they extend out at least 2 inches.

Teasing out the roots also fixes the problem of encircling roots. When plants have been in the nursery pot for a while, the roots grow in a circle, following the contour of the pot. Unless you straighten the roots, they'll continue growing in a circle after planting, eventually strangling the plant. Another way to handle encircling roots is to make inch-deep slices into the root ball.

Fill the space around the root ball with the amended soil mixture to the top of the hole. Hold the straightened roots horizontally while you place soil underneath them. Firm the soil in and around the roots with your hands, leaving no large air pockets and taking care not to break roots. Don't tamp the soil with your feet; such force will damage delicate roots and remove air spaces from the soil.

After planting container-grown shrubs, pay careful attention to watering. Don't let the soilless mix dry out until the roots have grown into the native soil.

**FIELD-GROWN PLANTS:** Generally, the soil around the roots of field-grown plants—those that are balled and burlapped—is similar to the amended soil of your planting bed. The roots are not pot-bound, so you do not need to untangle them before planting. Simply loosen the burlap.

When handling balled-and-burlapped shrubs, take care to avoid tearing roots loose from the stem. Pick up the plant by the ball, not the stem. Burlapped balls, especially those on camellias, need careful handling so the soil around the roots doesn't crumble when the burlap is removed. If the soil crumbles, roots will be exposed and often break. Constant contact with the soil is preferred because it is difficult for the fibrous root system of camellias, rhododendrons, and azaleas to gain contact with the soil in the garden. Soil that is sandy, heavily amended with organic matter, or dry is most likely to crumble.

If the root ball is dry, soak it in water before planting for 10 to 15 minutes or until air bubbles stop forming. For sandy and heavily amended soil, loosen the burlap carefully. If the root ball starts to fall apart, leave the burlap in place, retie it, and keep it tied until the root ball is in the hole and the hole is filled at least halfway with soil firmed around the bottom and lower sides of the ball. Then remove the twine and fold the burlap down as far as possible. If the root ball is firm and holds together in one piece, you can remove the burlap.

Treated (green) or plastic burlap must be completely removed. Any of this type of burlap left around the root ball will hinder root growth. If the root ball is crumbling, cut the plastic off.

Never leave burlap exposed above the soil. Like a wick, exposed burlap draws water away from roots as water evaporates from the burlap. Field-grown azaleas, rhododendrons, and camellias are often sold in fiber containers. If the root ball is not crumbly, remove the container. If it is, place the plant with the container in the hole. Break or tear off as

*For each shrub, prepare a 3- to 4-foot-wide planting area, amending soil well with organic matter. Build a berm around the shrub to direct water to the roots. Add mulch inside the berm to prevent the soil from drying too quickly.*

# PLANTING
*continued*

*A berm built around and 6 inches beyond the root ball helps prevent water runoff when water is applied by rain or irrigation.*

much of the container as possible. Then punch holes in the sides of what's left. The top of the container should not extend above soil level; it also wicks water away from roots.

## CREATE A WATER BASIN

Build a basin to hold water around the base of the shrub by patting unamended soil 6 inches outside the root ball into a 3- to 4-inch-high berm. The floor of the basin should be level with the soil surface outside the berm.

*A burlap windbreak-sunshade provides much-needed protection the first year after transplanting. This is especially important in winter and summer.*

If you didn't mix fertilizer into the soil when you prepared the planting bed, sprinkle a handful of an organic fertilizer, such as cottonseed or soybean meal, at the edge of the root ball. Then fill the basin with a loose, porous, 2- to 3-inch-deep layer of mulch, such as pine bark mini nuggets, oak leaves, composted wood chips, or pine needles. The more coarse and open the mulch is, the deeper you can apply it.

The next step in planting rhododendrons, azaleas, and camellias is to thoroughly water the entire planting area. Each shrub will take approximately 5 gallons of water. Watering helps settle the soil around the root ball and adds much-needed moisture.

## AFTERCARE

In the following weeks, properly watering the new plant is critical to its survival. The surrounding soil and root ball should be kept moist but not wet. Too much water kills roots just as effectively as not enough. Container-grown plants will need water on the root ball every two to three days in hot, sunny weather. In dry areas, they'll need water more often. The soil surrounding the ball may need water only once a week, so direct the water to the base of the shrubs, not the entire bed. Field-grown plants need water less often than container plants because the root ball is in soil, not a fast-drying soilless medium.

It is normal for new, tender growth to wilt on hot, sunny days, but when new growth remains wilted several hours after sundown, it's time to water. Irrigate deeply and only often enough to keep the root ball moist.

Compared with narrow-leaf evergreens like pines, broad-leaf evergreens transpire a lot of water through their leaves. A windbreak or sunshade can greatly reduce this demand for water and help camellias, azaleas, and rhododendrons become established in their new homes. It is best to surround the plant completely with a windbreak to moderate the wind, but a sunshade needs to provide protection only on three sides, all but the north.

Snow fence and burlap work well in temporary sunshades or windbreaks. To install one, pound four 1×2s into the soil around the shrubs, then tack burlap or snow fence to the 1×2s, leaving the top open to admit sunlight and rain. The 1×2s should be a foot from the plant—or at least far enough away that the plant doesn't touch the material. The shelter should be tall enough to shade the entire plant for most of the day.

# ROUTINE MAINTENANCE

Because broad-leaf evergreens lose moisture relatively faster than other plants, water is especially key to the growth of azaleas, rhododendrons, and camellias and must be supplied to the plants on a regular basis. In most situations, the plants require about 1 inch of water per week. During rainy seasons—such as winter and spring in many areas—the plants usually receive sufficient moisture from rainfall. Unfortunately, much of North America is subject to extremes of drought in summer, and supplemental water must be applied. The goal is to keep plant roots moist but not wet.

In the absence of natural rainfall, water is especially important during certain periods:

■ Immediately after planting and until the shrub is established in the landscape. (It can take several years for an adequate root system to develop.)

■ When plants are actively growing and flowering.

■ In fall so the plant goes into winter with adequate soil moisture.

■ Anytime the soil dries out enough to cause mature leaves to wilt during the day. (New, tender leaves often wilt, but this is not a problem if they resume a healthy, upright form soon after sunset.)

How much and how often plants need water varies in different soil types and in the proximity of other large plants such as trees. Sandy soils dry out quicker than loam or clay soil. Large trees deplete soil moisture quickly and to great depths. Rhododendrons, azaleas, and camellias in either of those situations will require more frequent watering.

*Water travels through soil in a bell-shaped curve. Take care to irrigate long enough to soak the entire root zone and the area surrounding it so roots grow into the amended soil. Apply water slowly and gently so it has time to soak in.*

## WHEN TO WATER

Newly transplanted shrubs must be monitored closely and watered so the root ball never dries out. If roots have grown enough to extend into the native soil, more moisture is available to the plants, but watering is still necessary every three to four days in hot weather, especially when plants are in bloom or sending out new growth. Water supplied by rain must be taken into consideration when deciding when to water. Although the amount varies somewhat, most plants need about 1 inch of water a week for best growth. The easiest way to determine when 1 inch of water has fallen is to place lidless, watertight containers with straight vertical sides, such as pet-food or tuna cans, near the planted area. Mark a 1-inch depth from the bottom of the can with a waterproof pen. When the container catches 1 inch of water, the plants have been adequately irrigated.

## WATERING METHODS

Small plantings can be adequately watered by hand, but the water flow out of the hose must be slow enough to prevent runoff, which does not reach the root zone. Applying water by hand usually results in inadequate watering. Use containers, as explained above, to measure the amount of water actually applied. Better yet, set up sprinklers so you won't be tempted to give up before the shrubs have received enough water.

Lawn sprinklers set to cover the planting are the best way to water because a sprinkler can be left on for extended periods of time to slowly soak the soil with little or no runoff. Sprinkling at night or in the early morning or evening results in less water lost to evaporation. When watering with sprinklers, be sure to check that no plants are outside the area hit by the water from the sprinklers.

Soaker hoses and drip irrigation systems are water-saving devices, but they require close monitoring. Check with your local extension service for advice on setting up and using these systems around shrubs.

## ROUTINE MAINTENANCE
*continued*

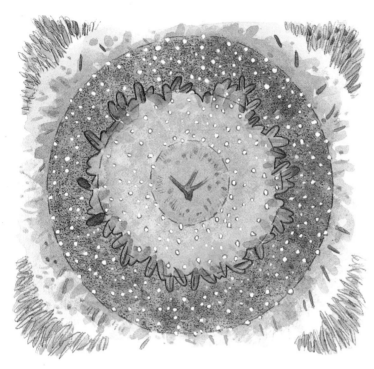

**Apply fertilizer from a point 1 foot inside the drip line to 1 foot outside the drip line. The drip line is the outside edge of the shrub.**

### FERTILIZING

Most rhododendrons, azaleas, and camellias are light feeders. Light feeders get their nutrients from the soil and therefore don't require as much fertilizer as other plants. However, fertilizing azaleas, rhododendrons, and camellias annually will ensure vigorous growth and high-quality blooms. Fertilize all three plants in spring, no later than June 1.

### MATERIALS

Where soil pH is above 6, apply only acid-producing fertilizers specially formulated for rhododendrons, azaleas, and camellias. Organic fertilizers such as cottonseed meal are also acid-forming. Acid-producing inorganic amendments include ammonium sulfate and sulfur-coated urea.

Both organic and inorganic fertilizers have pros and cons. In general, organic fertilizers provide small amounts of nutrients over time. Unlike quick-release inorganic nutrients, they seldom burn plants or cause salt buildup in the soil. But many products, such as cottonseed meal, vary in nutrient content. Processed organic fertilizers, such as Milorganite, have a more uniform analysis.

In contrast, nutrients in inorganic fertilizers are much more readily accessible to plant roots and are available in a wide range of concentrations. Inorganic fertilizers can be divided into two types: fast- and slow-release. Fast-release inorganic fertilizers, such as ammonium sulfate, are quickly available to the plant and do not provide an even flow of available nutrients over an extended period. Slow-release fertilizers, on the other hand, applied in spring can provide adequate nutrition for the entire growing season for well-mulched rhododendrons, azaleas, and camellias.

A mix of slow-release inorganic or organic fertilizers with a faster-release product gives azaleas, rhododendrons, and camellias a quick boost in spring and the long-term nutrients they require for the growing season. See page 35 for an abbreviated listing of materials and rates.

### SPECIFIC NEEDS

**RHODODENDRONS AND AZALEAS:** If the soil around rhododendrons and azaleas is adequately mulched—at least 3 inches deep—fertilizing is rarely necessary. In an acid soil, azaleas and rhododendrons are extremely efficient at extracting their own nutrients from natural sources. However, when mulches are not adequate to promote vigorous growth, a fertilizing schedule is desirable.

The time to fertilize azaleas and rhododendrons is from early spring, when the first azaleas start to bloom through early summer (no later than June 1). If plants are not growing well, are not filled out, or look unhealthy, additional fertilizer may be added after the plants go dormant in autumn but before the ground freezes.

For established plants in the landscape, apply fertilizers to the soil surface from a point halfway between the drip line (the outer edge of the foliage where the water runs off) and the trunk to a point about 2 feet outside the drip line. For newly planted rhododendrons and azaleas, sprinkle fertilizer over the root ball and only a few inches beyond.

**CAMELLIAS:** Camellias require more fertilizer than rhododendrons and azaleas do. However, when grown in a rich soil high in organic matter, they may not need fertilizer. Generally, camellias are fertilized once a year, in early spring before growth begins.

### WEEDING

The less competition from other plants, the better your azaleas, rhododendrons, and camellias will grow. Weeds not only compete for moisture and nutrients, they also block light from reaching desirable plants and they reduce air circulation.

Never dig around your azaleas, rhododendrons, or camellias to remove weeds; their shallow root systems will be damaged. Hand-pulling the weeds is the safest method. Pulling weeds when they are small causes much less disturbance to the soil and the camellia, rhododendron, and azalea plant roots.

Some herbicides, such as glyphosate, can be used safely around azaleas, rhododendrons, and camellias as long as they don't touch the shrubs' foliage. Never apply weed killers containing 2,4-D on or around these plants. Because herbicide labels occasionally change, carefully read the label before purchasing an herbicide to ensure that the product is still registered for use on azaleas, camellias, and rhododendrons.

*Good mulching materials for rhododendrons, azaleas, and camellias include, clockwise from upper left, composted fir or redwood sawdust, pine needles, pine bark mini nuggets, chopped oak leaves, bark chips, compost, and shredded pine bark.*

## MULCHING

A 3-inch-deep layer of mulch helps maintain soil moisture, control weeds, keep the soil cooler in summer, and delay freezing of the soil in early winter. It also prevents soil from packing down and crusting on the surface, resulting in better aeration and water penetration.

Mulch simply means a soil cover. It can be made of anything, but light, airy, organic mulches are typically associated with the natural habitats of rhododendrons, azaleas, and camellias. Thus, the ideal mulches for azaleas, camellias, and rhododendrons are loose, airy, and acid-forming. Pine bark, pine needles, oak leaves, wood chips, or other coarse materials are best. Avoid grass clippings, peat moss, maple leaves, or any other material that packs down or sheds water.

## WINTER PROTECTION

As long as you have selected a cultivar that is hardy in your area and planted it in a "favorite" azalea or rhododendron habitat, the same temporary shelter you installed as a sunshade or windbreak can be used to protect plants every winter and prevent them from desiccating. Use the shelter to shield plants from the sun and wind and thereby modify or slow temperature fluctuations for the first three years the plants are in the ground. However, if you plant camellias, azaleas, and rhododendrons outside of their cold-hardiness range, you must provide more elaborate protection.

## MATERIALS AND RATES FOR ESTABLISHED LANDSCAPE PLANTS

Before applying fertilizer, measure the square footage of the application area. In most instances, that is the area from 1 foot inside the drip line to 1 foot beyond the drip line.

| Fertilizer | Amount to Apply |
| --- | --- |
| Ammonium sulfate | 3.4 lbs. per 100 square feet |
| Commercial inorganic quick- and slow-release fertilizer mix, such as Azalea, Camellia, Rhododendron Food 16-2-3 | 1 cup per 40 square feet |
| Commercial 4-6-4 organic fertilizer, such as Holly Tone | 1 cup per foot of branch spread |
| Coated, slow-release fertilizers, such as Osmocote 18-6-12 | 1 teaspoon per square feet |
| Liquid fertilizer, such as Miracid 30-10-10 | 1 tablespoon per gallon per 10 square feet |
| Organic fertilizers, such as cottonseed meal | 3 cups per 100 square feet |

# TRANSPLANTING ESTABLISHED SHRUBS

Large shrubs are usually transplanted for several reasons. For example, you may want a landscape that looks established immediately after planting. Or a plant may have been improperly sited and outgrew its space, and you need to correct the mistake. Or you may finally have time to take care of a plant you were going to move years ago, when the plant was still small.

Regardless of the reason, moving a large plant is hard work, but it is not an impossible task. A small power tree spade simplifies the job. But because the shrubs are relatively shallow-rooted, they're fairly easy to dig and move by hand if you don't have access to such equipment and are in reasonably good shape. Here's how.

■ In early spring, one year before moving the shrub, prune the roots around the entire plant. Use a nursery spade (a spade with an 18-inch-long blade). Cut the roots by inserting the spade into the soil as deep as it will go.

How far out to cut the roots depends on the size of the shrub. A 6-foot plant should be moved with a 3- to 4-foot diameter ball, so measure 1½ to 2 feet from the trunk all around the shrub, then prune the roots about 3 inches inside this line. Mark the cutting line so you know where to dig the following fall or spring when you move the plant.

During the year between pruning the roots and moving the plant, many new roots will develop inside of the root-pruned area. This results in a compact, fibrous root ball with many feeder roots, which holds together well and ensures better survival when you finally move the plant.

The next year is when the work really begins. You'll probably want to line up a friend to help.

■ Prepare a hole to receive the plant (see page 30).

■ Dig a 12- to 18-inch-deep trench around the shrub. If the soil around the roots appears unstable as you work, wrap burlap around the ball. Secure the burlap with string or twine.

■ Next, begin to form the ball. Dig a wedge under the roots all the way around the shrub. Continue working around the shrub, extending the wedge further and further under the roots until the shrub is nearly free. Then push a digging iron or pry bar under the ball to undercut the roots all the way through. If necessary, wrap more burlap around the root ball and tie it tightly in place.

■ Pull on the trunk of the plant to tip it to one side. From the other side, pry up the ball far enough to slide a sheet of plywood or plastic (or a tarp) underneath it. Tip the plant back up. With the shrub on the sheet, drag it to its new location.

■ Pull the plywood over the hole and tip it up to slide the plant into the hole.

■ Finish up using the same techniques as for planting a field-grown azalea, camellia, or rhododendron (see page 31).

Aftercare of a transplanted shrub is the same as for new, nursery-grown shrubs. If the plant was healthy prior to moving, its chance of survival is high.

*If possible, bend up and tie the branches to make it easier to work around the plant.*

*Root-prune a large plant one year prior to moving it to a new location.*

*Slide the plant to its new location on a tarp, or a sheet of plastic or plywood.*

# GROOMING PLANTS

Gardeners groom plants to keep them healthy and attractive. Clipping off all dead leaves, branches, and blooms improves plant shape, and removes insect and disease damage.

## DEADHEADING

An important grooming task for camellias and rhododendrons is deadheading, which means to remove spent flower heads. Not only does deadheading groom the plant, it also ensures bountiful floral displays from year to year. Deadheading, if done as soon as the flowers fade, stimulates buds along the sides of the stem—the lateral buds—to form new shoots. It produces a more compact plant and heavier flower bud set for the following season.

Rhododendrons especially benefit from deadheading. Their large flower trusses are unsightly when spent. They're easy to remove. Simply hold the bottom of the truss between your thumb and forefinger, and bend it sideways. Be careful not to break off leaves or buds from the main stem in the process.

Because azaleas produce so many blossoms, spent flowers are usually left in place. Azaleas can be groomed by pinching tips to produce a more compact plant, removing dead wood, and pruning back tall, spindly shoots.

## DISBUDDING

One technique used on camellias but not on azaleas or rhododendrons is disbudding. Like deadheading, disbudding grooms plants and improves plant performance. Disbudding removes all but one or two terminal flower buds—the buds at the tip of the branch. Removing the other buds means the terminal bud has no competition, so it receives more nutrients and grows larger. Instead of many smaller flowers, the plant produces fewer, exceptionally large blossoms.

Typically, camellias are disbudded in fall, before they bloom. Plants grown under glass or in the house are the most likely candidates for disbudding because they are smaller and have fewer blooms. Outdoor plants are generally not disbudded because they are too large and have too many buds.

Gardeners who specialize in growing camellias sometimes use a technique called gibbing to increase flower size. Gibbing involves applying gibberellic acid to the cup left behind when disbudding. This practice is not often used by the home gardener. Contact your local chapter of the American Camellia Society for more detailed information.

*Removing the spent flower cluster, such as on this rhododendron, is called deadheading.*

*The shoot tip callouses over soon after the spent flower cluster has been removed.*

*A few weeks later, three new shoots have sprouted. The end result is a more compact plant bearing more flower buds.*

*To disbud camellias, remove all but the terminal bud. Simply snap the buds off one at a time with your thumb.*

# PRUNING

Pruning removes diseased and dead wood, shapes or thins a plant, rejuvenates an old plant, and reduces the size of an overgrown plant. If properly pruned at the nursery, a healthy, landscape-size plant whose mature size fits the site will require little pruning for several years after planting.

However, you may want to train your plant to fit a particular garden design role. Oriental gardens in particular rely on pruned azaleas to create an effect. To produce the typical oriental form and create the illusion of old age, selected branches are carefully removed to open the canopy and display the remaining branches and trunk.

Shearing can be used to shape evergreen azaleas into formal hedges. New shoots appear quickly and in great numbers, resulting in thick growth. Rhododendrons and deciduous azaleas do not respond well to shearing.

Pinching produces compact plants. That's because removing the terminal vegetative buds stimulates the lateral buds in leaf axils into growth. The result is two to five short shoots instead of one long shoot. Nursery staff pinch nearly all small plants to promote branching.

*Tip-pruning forces the growth of lateral buds, thus forming a more compact plant.*

*From left: Azalea buds break all along a stem, so prune anywhere. Prune elepidotes just above a whorl of buds. Lepidote and camellia buds break only in leaf axils, so prune just above a leaf.*

## RHODODENDRONS AND AZALEAS

How much pruning and the method to use depend on several factors, including the type of plant, the desired effect, and the plant's age. For tools, you'll need lopping shears, a pruning saw, and hand pruners.

**LEPIDOTES AND AZALEAS:** Azaleas and lepidote rhododendrons don't usually require yearly pruning except to remove an occasional vigorous shoot that reduces the garden appeal of the plant. They can, however, be pruned to train them to grow in a particular direction.

You can prune lepidote rhododendrons and azaleas virtually anywhere on a stem, cutting them as far back as desired to reduce the plant's size. This works because "invisible" buds dot the entire length of the stems. When these invisible, or adventitious, buds break, new shoots develop in spots where they're not normally expected, such as between leaves instead of at leaf axils or stem tips.

After azaleas and lepidote rhododendrons are pruned, new shoots will usually form within a month wherever an adventitious bud breaks. The shoots can appear a few inches below the cut or all the way back to the ground. These shoots are capable of flowering the following season if they're pruned immediately after flowering in early spring.

**ELEPIDOTE RHODODENDRONS:** Elepidote rhododendrons should be pruned in early spring immediately after they bloom because they are slow to send out new shoots. The plants require a long period of growth for the new shoots to mature and harden off before

## TIP

Many plant diseases, such as dieback, can be spread when pruning. When pruning affected plants, sterilize pruners, and all other cutting tools used on the plants between each cut. To sterilize, dip the tools into rubbing alcohol (90%) or a mixture of 1 part bleach to 9 parts water.

**REJUVENATING OVERGROWN SHRUBS**

*Gangly, overgrown shrub with new growth at base*

*All but new growth pruned away*

*Regrowth on pruned stubs of an overgrown shrub*

winter and to set flower buds for the following season.

Most elepidote rhododendrons do not have buds the full length of their stems, only at the tips. Usually, several buds grow in a whorl around the end of a stem. Prune elepidotes just above one of these whorls of buds. If you want to considerably shorten a stem and can't find a whorl, prune the stem at any point. After new shoots sprout, prune off the stubs. Some elepidote cultivars have leaves and buds 1 or 2 inches down the stem. If pruned below these older leaves, the plants could lose a season of bloom.

## CAMELLIAS

The main reason for pruning camellias is to remove diseased or weak branches and leggy growth. Although not harmful, leggy growth is unattractive. You should also thin plants occasionally to prevent overcrowding and renew plant vigor.

Pruning helps improve flowering. The best blooms are produced on vigorous, small- to medium-size plants. As a plant grows and matures, it develops more growing points so it sets more flower buds. This reduces shoot vigor, and individual flowers tend to be smaller. Although pruning improves vigor and flower size, too much pruning may increase vigor but result in fewer flowers.

Like elepidotes, camellias have no adventitious buds. Unlike them, though, camellias have leaves farther down on the stem, and every leaf axil has buds. Pruning forces buds into growth for several inches below the cut.

The best time to prune camellias is when the plants have stopped blooming but before they start putting out new growth.

Prune fall-blooming camellias in early spring, after the danger of frost is past.

To thin camellias, cut the stems back to a branch or to the trunk. Do not leave stubs. Also, remove twigs that have only one weak terminal bud and no side buds. Weak buds are less plump and have poor growth compared with other buds. Vigorous shoots have up to three well-developed terminal leaf buds and side buds. As a general rule, cut out branches that tend to grow inward, for they will be shaded out in later years. Remove all dead and dying twigs.

## REJUVENATING OVERGROWN SHRUBS

Azaleas, rhododendrons, and camellias outgrow their allotted space in the landscape and lose vigor as they age. Prune them severely to give them new life. This usually results in more compact plants.

There are two methods of rejuvenating azaleas and rhododendrons. The first is to remove all branches to within a foot of the soil level; the other is to prune a third of the branches down to stubs each year for three years. If the shrub has small shoots or leaves growing near the ground, the all-at-once system works well. If no shoots are sprouting from the ground at the base of the shrub, thinning out one-third of the branches at a time is better. This method lets more light into the plant interior, which may stimulate new shoot growth.

To rejuvenate a camellia or to reduce it to manageable size, cut back each branch to a vigorous shoot. If no good shoots can be found, remove a large portion of the weaker branches and wait to see which parts of the shrub put out new growth.

# PROPAGATING

*Spread seeds evenly over the surface of the growing medium. Do not cover azalea or rhododendron seeds.*

*When seedlings develop true leaves, pry under the roots and lift them for transplanting. Pick up the seedling by its leaves.*

*Gently firm the peat moss-and-perlite planting medium around the seedling roots and water in.*

A rewarding way to gain more azaleas, rhododendrons, and camellias is by propagating them from stem cuttings.

## CUTTINGS

Propagating plants from stem cuttings produces new plants that are identical to the parent. To ensure that taking the cutting doesn't injure the parent plant, you should use good pruning practices and not leave stubs.

Evergreen azalea cuttings root well no matter when you take them—from a month after flowering until fall. But for the other plants, timing is critical.

Take deciduous azalea cuttings in early spring when shoots are soft (they're called softwood cuttings). Any later and they won't root. However, native deciduous azaleas are difficult to propagate from cuttings and may not produce new plants.

Make rhododendron cuttings from the current year's growth when the color of the new leaves has reached the same intensity of green as that of year-old leaves. Some lepidote and elepidote rhododendrons root better from hardwood cuttings. These are taken in fall through January from stems that are mature and rigid. Camellia cuttings root best when the wood is semihard (after the new growth has firmed up but before it has become rigid).

## STEPS

First, select a firm but pliable stem from the current season's growth. Cut it off at its base.

Trim azalea and rhododendron cuttings to 2½ to 2¾ inches long and camellias to three buds long. Remove all but the top four leaves.

When propagating elepidote rhododendrons or camellias, trim the top half of the remaining leaves. On azaleas, simply pinch the tip of the stem. Finally, cut ½-inch-long lengthwise slits on each side of the cuttings at their bases, just deep enough to expose the inner wood.

After preparing the cuttings, fill a flat or pot with a mix of 50 percent sphagnum peat moss and 50 percent perlite. Dip each cutting in rooting hormone (the chart on page 41 details which to use). Insert the stems into the soil mix in 1-inch-deep holes made with a pencil or chopstick. Camellia cuttings should be inserted deep enough to cover the bottom bud. Firm the medium around the cuttings, then cover the flat with plastic to keep the humidity high and place it under artificial lights or outdoors in a shady spot.

When the cuttings develop a 2-inch root ball, transplant them into pots filled with a mix of peat and perlite. Azalea cuttings root in about four weeks, rhododendrons in about 12 weeks, and camellias in 10 to 12 weeks.

## PROPAGATING A RHODODENDRON FROM CUTTINGS

**Step 1** *To make a rhododendron cutting, select a new stem that is firm but just pliable enough to bend. Cut the stem at its base.*

**Step 2** *Remove the lower leaves from the cutting. On elepidote rhododendrons, clip off the top halves of the remaining leaves.*

**Step 3** *Dip the base of the cutting into rooting hormone. See the box below for which rooting hormone to use.*

**Step 4** *Make a hole in the potting mix to keep the hormone from being scraped off, then insert the cutting.*

**Step 5** *Water the cutting (or prewet the potting mix). Cover the container with plastic to hold in moisture.*

**Step 6** *The cutting is ready to transplant when it has developed a 2-inch root ball.*

Overwinter the young transplants inside under lights, or in a cold frame. Move them to the garden the following year.

## GROWING FROM SEED

**RHODODENDRONS AND AZALEAS:** Seed propagation is an accepted nursery practice for some species of rhododendrons and azaleas, but it does not produce exact copies of the parents. Propagating by seed is the way to produce new and different cultivars.

Rhododendrons and azaleas set many tiny brown seeds in elongated, cone-shaped pods. The pods ripen in autumn, turning brittle and splitting open. Use only seed from hand-pollinated species to ensure purity and plants with similar characteristics.

Collect seeds in fall as soon as they turn brown, before the capsules split. Start the seeds in flats or pots filled with sphagnum peat moss. Moisten the moss thoroughly, then squeeze it dry before filling the flat. Fresh seed—less than one year old when you sow it—has a 90 percent germination rate. The rate drops to 50 percent after the first year.

Seeds germinate in approximately two to four weeks at a temperature of 65° to 70° F. Keep seedlings indoors under lights for the first winter, water them carefully, and fertilize with a liquid fertilizer for acid-loving plants. Apply fertilizer at one-third the labeled strength every third watering. Water when the medium starts to dry. After the first true leaves form, transplant the seedlings from flats into pots.

The next spring after frost danger is past, transplant the seedlings into larger pots in a 50 percent organic soil mix. Move them to a cold frame until the following spring. Then they can be grown in nursery beds for one more year before being moved to the garden.

**CAMELLIAS:** To grow camellias from seed, use the same techniques with these differences: Seeds germinate at 70° to 85° F. File or cut through the seed coat before sowing so moisture can enter. Plant seeds ¾ inch deep. At transplanting, pinch off the tip of the seedling's taproot for a more fibrous root system.

### ROOTING HORMONE

| Plant | Strength to Use | Product |
|---|---|---|
| Camellias | 0.1% | Indolebutyric Acid (Rootone F) |
| Deciduous azaleas | | None needed |
| Evergreen azaleas | 0.1% | Indolebutyric Acid (Rootone F) |
| Rhododendrons | 0.8% to 1.3% | Indolebutyric Acid (Hormodin #3) |

# DEALING WITH PROBLEMS

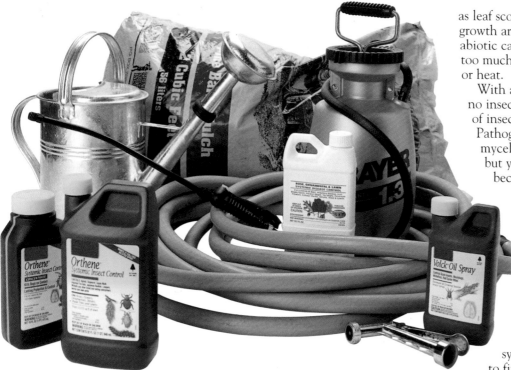

*The arsenal for fighting problems includes mulch, hoses and sprinklers, and pruners because a healthy plant is less likely to suffer from problems. You'll also want to have some pesticides on hand, including triadimefon, acephate, and horticultural oil.*

Rhododendrons, azaleas, and camellias can suffer from three types of problems. Two of these, insects and diseases, are caused by biotic, or living, organisms. The third—physiological problems—results from environmental stress factors such as sun damage, drought, overly wet soil, nutrient excesses or deficiencies, physical damage, and other nonliving, or abiotic, causes.

It is extremely important to diagnose whether a problem is biotic or abiotic so you can apply the proper treatment. Determining the difference between the "symptoms" and the "signs" of a problem is the first step.

A symptom is a plant's reaction to a causal agent. Typical symptoms of distress include poor foliage color, leaf scorch, dieback, slow growth, and, in extreme cases, death. Examine symptoms carefully because many causal factors result in the same symptoms.

A sign is the actual presence of the causal organism, such as the fungus, insect, or mite that is creating difficulties. Although signs ease diagnosis, you still must determine whether they are the cause of the problem or a secondary result of the original cause.

## IDENTIFYING THE PROBLEM

**ABIOTIC DISORDERS:** These result from poor cultural practices or from the wrong match between cultivar and site. Such things as leaf scorch, yellowing, and poor growth are frequently traced to abiotic causes, such as moisture—too much or too little—or to sun or heat.

With abiotic problems, there are no insects nor any damage typical of insects, such as notched leaves. Pathogenic fungal spores and mycelia aren't present either, but you might see fungal signs, because a weakened plant can become susceptible to a secondary fungus. Established rhododendrons, azaleas, and camellias growing in well-drained, high-organic soils seldom exhibit abiotic problems. But recently transplanted shrubs may show symptoms of stress for three to five years and need special care to prevent the abiotic disorders.

**DISEASES:** Generally caused by a fungus, diseases show up on the plant as disfigured leaves, stems, or flowers, as circular or irregular spots or brown edges on leaves, or as branch dieback. Diseases are identified by the presence of spores (the fruiting bodies of fungi) or mycelia ("roots" of the fungus). Spores often resemble dark specks of dirt; mycelia look cottony. But both may be impossible to see without a magnifying glass or microscope.

Sometimes the only way to diagnose a fungal infection is to send affected plant parts to a plant pathology lab or diagnosis center allied with a university. The lab will culture the disease and make recommendations as to control. Contact your local extension office to find such a lab.

**INSECTS, MITES, AND SLUGS:** Plant damage by insects, mites, and slugs is quickly discovered because of the obvious physical damage. Size, shape, and location of holes on leaves often help identify the pest.

## AVOIDING PROBLEMS

When poor cultural practices weaken plants, insects and diseases generally follow. Healthy, vigorously growing plants resist many insects and diseases. If nothing else, they outgrow the problem. Another way to avoid problems is to select insect- and disease-resistant cultivars.

# ABIOTIC DISORDERS

Several physiological or abiotic disorders can create symptoms on azaleas, camellias, and rhododendrons. The following are the major physiological disorders you are likely to encounter.

*Iron chlorosis shows up as yellow leaves with dark veins.*

## IRON CHLOROSIS

**AFFECTED PLANTS:** Rhododendrons, azaleas, and camellias.

**SYMPTOMS:** Some of the leaves are pale green to yellow. The newest leaves may be completely yellow, with only the veins and the tissue next to the veins remaining green.

**ANALYSIS:** Iron chlorosis is a common problem in acid-loving plants. It is caused by a deficiency of iron in plant tissues. Although soil is seldom deficient in iron, the iron is often in an insoluble form that is not available to the plant, especially when the pH is 7 or higher. Plants located near concrete paths or walls, especially in naturally alkaline areas, are likely to develop iron chlorosis.

**TREATMENT:** Increase soil acidity by adding iron sulfate, ammonium sulfate, or sulfur. After each application, check the soil pH and add more chemical if needed. Page 35 provides a chart of the rates to use for these materials, but you should follow the directions on the product's label as well. You can also mulch soil with leaf mold or pine needles and use a fertilizer formulated for acid-loving plants. If the problem is severe, spray the foliage with chelated iron.

## SALT BURN

**AFFECTED PLANTS:** Rhododendrons, azaleas, and camellias.

**SYMPTOMS:** Leaf edges turn brown and brittle. Browning usually occurs first on older leaves, which are the lowest leaves on a branch. This distinguishes the problem from windburn, which develops on young, exposed leaves closest to the branch tip.

**ANALYSIS:** Salt burn occurs when excess salts in the soil are taken up by the plant and accumulate in the leaves. This problem is most common in areas of long-term or short-term low rainfall and also where too much fertilizer has been applied. Salt burn can occur in acid or alkaline soil. It can also occur in plants growing in poorly drained soil or in containers.

**TREATMENT:** The damage will not disappear from affected leaves, but injury can be avoided in the future. In areas of low rainfall, leach accumulated salts from the soil with an occasional, once-a-month, heavy irrigation (apply more than an inch of water). Also improve soil drainage to allow salts to leach away more readily. Flush excess salts from container soils by watering the plant heavily several times in a row. Do not overfertilize, and water thoroughly after fertilizing to prevent salt buildup.

*Salt burn, which turns leaf margins brown and dry, affects older leaves first.*

## WINDBURN, SUNBURN, AND WINTER INJURY

**AFFECTED PLANTS:** Rhododendrons, azaleas, and camellias.

**SYMPTOMS:** Young, exposed leaves turn brown and dry, especially around their leaf edges and near tips. One side of the plant may look healthy while the other side looks sick.

**ANALYSIS:** The shrub is planted in a windy or sunny location or is growing in a cold climate where cold, dry, windy days are common. Excess sun and heat can cause the same symptoms. Windburn and winter injury are common on plants growing in windswept locations. When winter temperatures drop below freezing, strong winds cause leaves to lose moisture more rapidly than the root system can replace it. The damage may not appear for several weeks. Leaf burn also occurs on exceptionally windy, dry summer days or in excessive sun in hot climates.

**TREATMENT:** If damage is localized, prune away affected limbs. To prevent further damage, plant shrubs in locations protected from wind and sun or install temporary burlap sunshades and windbreaks around the plant. Shrubs should be well-watered during hot, windy weather. Water in late fall or during winter, if necessary, to ensure adequate soil moisture.

*Brown, crisp edges on young rhododendron leaves usually indicate sunburn or windburn.*

# INSECTS

This notching of a rhododendron leaf edge is typical of the damage that adult weevils (inset) cause.

Dark shiny spots on the underside of a leaf are a definitive symptom of azalea lace bug.

## LACE BUG

**AFFECTED PLANTS:** Rhododendrons and azaleas.

**SYMPTOMS:** Leaves are speckled white or yellow and green. Symptoms are similar to those from mites.

**SIGNS:** Look for ⅛-inch-long, spiny, wingless larvae or brownish adult insects with large, clear, lacy wings. In the absence of actual insects, look for hard, shiny, black droplets on the undersides of damaged leaves. This is their excrement.

**ANALYSIS:** Lace bugs suck sap from the undersides of leaves and leave black drops of excrement. They are more prevalent in sunny conditions than in shade. Damage is unsightly and reduces plant vigor. Lace bugs are the most common insect problem on azaleas.

**TREATMENT:** When you first see the bugs, spray an insecticide containing acephate. Take care to coat all of the leaves. Repeat in 14 days. A third application may be necessary. Insecticidal soap and horticultural oils are about 80 percent effective, but the insects must be hit with the spray. Acephate is systemic in the plant, so it is not necessary for the spray to contact the insects. It can give 100 percent control. A relatively new product, imidacloprid (Merit), is also effective.

## BLACK VINE WEEVIL AND STRAWBERRY ROOT WEEVIL

**AFFECTED PLANTS:** Rhododendrons and azaleas.

**SYMPTOMS:** Leaf margins are scalloped or notched; leaves may be yellowed, drooping, or curled. Look for areas at the base of the stem where the bark has been chewed.

**SIGNS:** You may find ¼- to ½-inch-long legless "grubs" in the soil. If you inspect plants at night, you may see black or grayish insects with ¼- to ⅜-inch-long snouts on the leaves. These are the adult weevils.

**ANALYSIS:** The most damage is caused by the grubs, which are the larvae of the weevils, by feeding on the roots of the plants. Adult weevils lay eggs close to the bases of stems during summer, and the hatching larvae burrow into the soil. They injure the roots and often girdle the stem by cutting off the plant's nutrients; they may cause wilting and death.

**TREATMENT:** Discard severely injured plants. When you see adult weevils or when you first see notchings in the leaves, spray foliage and soil around adjacent healthy plants with an insecticide that contains acephate (Orthene). Repeat two or three times at three-week intervals. Sometimes, five or six treatments from May through September are needed to achieve complete control.

## RHODODENDRON BORER

**AFFECTED PLANTS:** Rhododendrons and azaleas.

**SYMPTOMS:** Dime-size spots dot leaves. Shoots at the outer edge of the plant may wilt. Bark along the main stem and side branches flakes away, revealing tunnels and holes.

**SIGNS:** None; borer resides within trunk.

**ANALYSIS:** Rhododendron borers are the larvae of a moth common in the Atlantic Coast states. The yellowish-white caterpillar is ½ inch long. It hatches from eggs laid on the

*Rhododendron borer larvae (inset) tunnel through the plant, starting at the base of the trunk.*

bark and burrows into the wood, working its way down the trunk and along the branches.
**TREATMENT:** Once inside the wood, borers are almost impossible to control. The only remedy is to prune wilted branches. Prevent the pest early in the season by spraying or painting the trunk with an insecticide containing lindane, acephate, or imidacloprid to kill hatching larvae before they burrow. Repeat three more times at two-week intervals.

## SCALE

**AFFECTED PLANTS:** Camellias and occasionally rhododendrons and azaleas.
**SYMPTOMS:** Leaves turn yellow and branches die back. The plant may die.

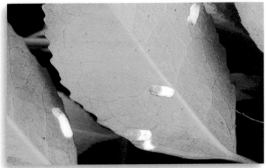

*White, gray, or brown bumps on the undersides of camellia leaves are the first sign of a scale infestation.*

**SIGNS:** White, yellow, brown, gray, or reddish bumps appear on the stems, branches, and leaves. The bumps can be scraped or picked off; undersides are usually soft.
**ANALYSIS:** Many scale species attack azaleas and rhododendrons. Tea scale is the most common and probably most damaging pest of camellias. Scales lay eggs on leaves or bark in spring to midsummer. The young scales crawl to various parts of the plant, then settle in and feed on plant sap. Once they find a permanent spot, their legs atrophy and a hard, crusty or waxy shell grows over the body.
**TREATMENT:** Spray with malathion or acephate when crawlers are active, usually in June.

The following year in early spring, before new growth begins, spray branches and trunk with horticultural oil to control overwintering stages.

## SPIDER MITE

**AFFECTED PLANTS:** Azaleas, rhododendrons, and camellias.
**SYMPTOMS:** Leaves become discolored and distorted, stippled yellow or bronze. There may be fine webs on the lower surfaces of leaves.
**SIGNS:** For positive identification, hold a sheet of white paper underneath an affected leaf and tap the leaf sharply. Green, red, or yellow specks the size of pepper grains will drop to the paper. If they are mites, they'll crawl around.
**ANALYSIS:** Spider mites damage plants by sucking sap. Mites are active throughout the growing season and are especially favored by hot, dry weather. Once infestations occur, their effects are devastating, so administer controls as early as possible.
**TREATMENT:** Spray with a mitacide containing fenbutatin-oxide (Vendex). Repeat the application if the plant becomes visibly reinfested. Be sure to spray on the undersides of the leaves. You can also keep mite populations down by hosing plants with strong jets of water to dislodge webs and mites. To be effective, however, this must be an ongoing procedure. Insecticidal soap and horticultural oil are also effective.

*The discolored leaves on this azalea are signs of spider mite infestation. Leaves sometimes become distorted as well.*

## WHITEFLY

**AFFECTED PLANTS:** Rhododendrons, azaleas, and camellias.
**SYMPTOMS:** Leaves are mottled and yellow. A sticky substance called honeydew coats the leaves, and a black sooty mold may grow on the honeydew.
**SIGNS:** White, $\frac{1}{12}$-inch-long, winged insects appear on the undersides of leaves. When the plant is touched, the insects rise up in a cloud.
**ANALYSIS:** Winged adults lay eggs on the underside of leaves. Flat, semi-transparent, pale green larvae are the size of pinheads. Both larvae and adults suck sap and secrete a sugary fluid called honeydew.
**TREATMENT:** Spray with an insecticide containing acephate, malathion, or diazinon. Repeat the spray two more times at intervals of 10 days. Thoroughly spray all surfaces of the leaves.

*Whiteflies are visible on this plant. Shaking the branch causes the small white insects to temporarily fly away.*

# DISEASES

Because a particular disease can be highly localized to an area, check with nearby nursery staff or your county extension office to learn which diseases are prevalent in your region. The diseases listed here are known to attack camellias, rhododendrons, and azaleas. Control them by improving air circulation or applying preventive sprays before a serious attack occurs.

## AZALEA PETAL BLIGHT

**AFFECTED PLANTS:** Azaleas.
**SYMPTOMS:** Tiny, circular spots form on the flower petals of azaleas. The spots are pale or whitish on colored flowers and rust-colored on white flowers. They enlarge, forming irregular patches, until the entire flower collapses. Petals feel slimy. Infected flowers dry up and cling to the plant.
**SIGNS:** Small, dark, semicircular pellets—the resting stage of the fungus—may be found on petals.
**ANALYSIS:** Azalea petal blight is a serious fungal disease of azaleas in humid coastal regions of the United States. Affected flowers decay rapidly. In early spring, the dark pellets produce spores that infect flowers. The disease is especially destructive in wet weather.
**TREATMENT:** Spray with a fungicide containing triadimefon (Bayleton), chlorothalonil (Daconil), or triforine (Funginex) as soon as flower buds show color. Test the spray on a few flowers before treating the entire plant; on some varieties, it may discolor the blooms.

Triadimefon applied just as the flower buds show color may be the best control in a dry spring. Repeat the application in 10 days during a wet spring.

The earliest-blooming azaleas do not contract this disease because the ambient temperature must reach 62° F before infection can occur. All plants that flower with and after the azalea 'Martha Hitchcock' need protection. Clean up and destroy litter around the base of plants and pick off diseased flowers, if feasible. To prevent infection next year, begin spraying when the flowers first start to show color—as soon as the buds open slightly so you can see a hint of the colored petals. Before flowering begins, spray the

*Petal blight infects flowers as soon as buds show color.*

ground under the shrub with a fungicide containing the chemical PCNB.

## CAMELLIA FLOWER BLIGHT

**AFFECTED PLANTS:** Camellias.
**SYMPTOMS:** Tan or brown spots or blotches spread across the flower; the whole flower may turn brown and drop from the plant. Affected portions of the flower develop darkened veins in a netted pattern.

*Browning of the camellia flower is caused by the flower blight fungus.*

**SIGNS:** None
**ANALYSIS:** This disease is caused by a fungus. Spores are carried to new flowers in late winter to early spring. If moisture is present, the fungus infects the flowers, which may turn completely brown within 48 hours.
**TREATMENT:** Pick off and destroy infected blossoms, and rake up and destroy old leaves, flowers, and plant debris. If camellia flower blight is especially severe in your area, protect the flowers with a spray containing mancozeb as soon as they begin to show color. Repeat every three days to protect new flowers.

## BOTRYOSPHAERIA DIEBACK

**AFFECTED PLANTS:** Rhododendrons and azaleas.
**SYMPTOMS:** Branches die on an otherwise healthy plant. Leaves become dull green, then turn brown.
**SIGNS:** None
**ANALYSIS:** Infection takes place through wounds. Heat and drought stress increase

*Flagging of leaves on a single branch of this rhododendron is the first symptom of botryosphaeria dieback.*

incidence of this fungal disease. Plants in full sun are most affected. Some species and cultivars are resistant; others are severely infected.

**TREATMENT:** This disease is difficult to control in the landscape. Immediately remove all dying branches below discolored wood. Disinfect pruners between each cut. Selection of resistant cultivars, such as yakushimanum hybrids and species and 'Caroline' offers the best control.

## LEAF GALL

**AFFECTED PLANTS:** Azaleas and rhododendrons. Some cultivars are resistant.
**SYMPTOMS:** Leaves, flower parts, seedpods, or branches swell. On branches, the disease may appear as a canker; elsewhere it develops into galls.

**SIGNS:** As the galls mature and reach the reproductive stage, a white coating of spores appears on their outer surfaces.
**ANALYSIS:** Leaf gall is caused by a fungus, which can overwinter in the stem or in leaf galls on stems and leaves.
**TREATMENT:** Handpick and remove galls before the spores develop. Because the fungus can overwinter and cause infection the following year, destroy the galls. You can throw them in the garbage or bury them, but don't put them on the compost pile.

*Leaf galls distort the tissue of leaves, stems, flowers, and seedpods.*

## POWDERY MILDEW

**AFFECTED PLANTS:** Deciduous azaleas and, in some areas, rhododendrons.
**SYMPTOMS:** Infected new growth becomes stunted and distorted. Leaves may discolor and die.
**SIGNS:** A grayish-white, powdery material consisting of fungal strands and spores covers leaves, stems, or flowers.

**ANALYSIS:** Powdery mildew is caused by a fungus, which commandeers plant nutrients for itself and distorts and discolors leaves.
**TREATMENT:** Spray with a fungicide containing triadimefon. Rake up and destroy plant debris. For best control, grow mildew-resistant cultivars. Many new mildew-resistant deciduous azaleas are available, including 'Satan', 'Sham's Yellow', 'Yellow Pom Pom', 'Crimson Tide', and 'Red Pom Pom'.

*Powdery mildew produces a white dusting of fungus on the leaves.*

## ROOT ROT

**AFFECTED PLANTS:** Rhododendrons, azaleas, and camellias.
**SYMPTOMS:** Young leaves turn yellow and wilt. Dead leaves remain attached to the plant and roll up along the midrib.
**SIGNS:** Cutting or peeling back the bark of a stem at ground level reveals tissue with a dark discoloration. There is a distinct line between diseased dark wood and healthy white wood. The plant will probably die.
**ANALYSIS:** Root rot is caused by soil fungi, generally phytopthora, that infect and destroy roots. Sometimes the fungi work their way up the stem. If they girdle the stem, the plant wilts and dies. Wet conditions favor the spread of the disease, which is most common in low-lying or poorly drained soil.
**TREATMENT:** Applying a fungicide containing metalaxyl to the soil helps suppress the problem. Follow label directions. Preventive measures include planting in locations with well-drained soil and good air circulation. Plants grown in raised beds are less susceptible to the disease. Where root rot is a problem, plant species or varieties that are resistant to root rot, such as sasanqua camellias or 'Caroline' and 'English Roseum' rhododendrons.

*When phytopthora root rot attacks, the entire plant wilts even when soil moisture is adequate.*

# ENCYCLOPEDIA OF RHODODENDRONS, AZALEAS & CAMELLIAS

*Small-statured azaleas fit right in among perennials. Here, a deciduous azalea blooms with tulips, hosta, and hakonechloa.*

Because rhododendrons, azaleas, and camellias are long-lived and often develop into large, woody shrubs, they are used as permanent plantings. When you make your selections, you need to carefully consider the characteristics of the plants and how they will grow in your garden, especially when they reach full size. This encyclopedia of hundreds of these plants will help you.

The first and most important factor in choosing plants for your landscape is whether the plants are adapted to your climate and the conditions within your garden. Also evaluate your landscape qualities and needs and the growth habits of the plants you are considering. The effect of a loose, open, upright growth habit is entirely different from that of a dense, spreading growth habit, but you may need more ground cover than screening depending on your land.

Pay attention to the plant's mature size and how quickly it will grow to that size. The sizes given in this encyclopedia are approximate. Plants in mild climates, such as that of the Pacific Northwest, enjoy a longer growing season and tend to grow a little larger than those in colder areas.

Consider how the color of the flowers will blend with other flower and foliage colors in your garden. Your plant will not have flowers much of the year, so think about the quality of the foliage. Take into account the color, texture, and shape of the leaves; the appearance of new growth; and, in the case of azaleas and rhododendrons, the indumentum, or downiness, on the undersides of the leaves.

Purchase named plants from a reliable local garden center or mail-order nursery. Often, plants sold only by color name rather than cultivar name may be seedlings that are inferior to selected named cultivars or varieties.

The entries in this encyclopedia describe the individual plants in detail. This is not an exhaustive list of plants, as there are several thousand hybrids.

Only passing reference is made to terms that may be unfamiliar to you. For example: Iron Clad refers to the old hybrids from England, which are cold-hardy and easy to grow. Also, plant hybridizers' names are mentioned

*'Lem's Cameo', an elepidote rhododendron, is an eye-catcher as it brightens up the garden.*

but may mean little to the average gardener, so they will not be expanded upon here.

You will find, however, many of the most widely available and choicest plants to aid you in filling your garden needs. If you live in an area where rhododendrons, azaleas, or camellias will grow, you're sure to see a great number of plants that will perfectly suit your particular climate and landscape.

## ENCYCLOPEDIA ORGANIZATION

The encyclopedia is divided into three sections: rhododendrons, azaleas, and camellias. Each of these sections is further divided into subsections, most of which contain lists of hybrids. The hybrid entries are listed alphabetically by their cultivar names, such as 'Scintillation' or 'Pink Perfection'. These are the names you would ask for when visiting a local nursery or ordering from a mail-order company. If you know the name of a particular species or hybrid, use the index to find the plant.

**PLANT DESCRIPTION:** Each entry describes the plant's most noteworthy characteristics. In most cases, you'll find flower color and size plus details about leaf size and shape, growth habit, mature plant size, and cold hardiness. Sometimes hybridizers' names or groups of hybrids are included in the description of a particular plant.

**ADAPTATION MAPS:** To help you quickly pinpoint cultivars that are right for your region, the entry for each plant or group of plants refers you to one of the adaptation maps below. These maps are divided into three areas.

**AREA 1 (BLUE ON THE MAP):** Well-adapted. The plant can be grown outdoors with a minimum of care. The plant may need supplemental watering and fertilizing, but climate protection is not required for the plant's survival. However, protection may help extend the growing season.

**AREA 2 (RED ON THE MAP):** Marginally adapted. The plant can be grown outdoors, but it will require more care than well-adapted plants. Climate protection may be required for survival.

**AREA 3 (UNCOLORED PART OF THE MAP):** Not adapted. Does not survive or produce flowers outdoors. May be grown as a greenhouse plant or as a container plant that is overwintered indoors.

*Camellias are at their best as understory plants, especially with this cherry tree in flower at the same time.*

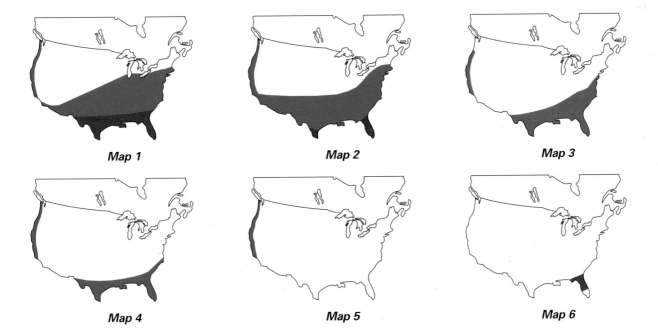

*Map 1*

*Map 2*

*Map 3*

*Map 4*

*Map 5*

*Map 6*

# RHODODENDRONS

## HEIGHTS

**DWARF**
Under 2 feet

**LOW**
2 to 4 feet

**MEDIUM**
4 to 6 feet

**TALL**
Over 6 feet

Spectacular flowers in nearly every color and versatility in the landscape endear rhododendrons to gardeners everywhere. They are divided into three categories: hybrids (lepidote and elepidote), species, and vireyas. Plant heights fall into the categories at left and are included in all entries. To adapt the bloom season times at right, note that in mild climates, early-blooming plants may begin to flower by the end of February. In cold climates, they bloom much later. Awards mentioned are from the American Rhododendron Society.

## BLOOM TIMES

**VE: VERY EARLY**
About 1 month before last killing frost

**E: EARLY**
About 10 days before last killing frost

**M: MIDSEASON**
About 2 weeks after last killing frost

**LM: LATE MIDSEASON**
About 3 weeks after last killing frost

**L: LATE**
About 4 weeks after last killing frost

## Lepidote Hybrids

The leaves of these relatively hardy plants feature small dotlike scales; many put on a foliage show from summer to winter.

**APRIL ROSE:** Double, slightly fragrant, funnel-shaped pink blooms and reddish leaves in fall highlight 'April Rose'. Low to medium, cold-hardy to –25° F. Blooms M. See Map 1.

**BLUE DIAMOND:** 'Blue Diamond' has 1½-inch-wide, light bluish-tinted-violet flowers. It is a dense, compact plant that grows best in the Northwest and in full sun. 'Blue Ridge', a new, similar cultivar, is more cold-hardy. Low, hardy to –5° F. Blooms E–M. See Map 2.

*'Blue Diamond'*

**CORNELL PINK:** Often called an azalea, it is a cultivar of the rhododendron *R. mucronulatum*. The flowers are a true pink. Blooms open to form flattened 1½- to 2-inch-wide trumpets. This early-flowering shrub is deciduous, with small leaves. It is often used with forsythia to create an interesting early display of color. Medium to tall, hardy to –25° F. Blooms VE. See Map 1.

**DORA AMATEIS:** This recipient of the Award of Excellence has 2-inch-wide white flowers, lightly spotted with green in the blotch, and borne in small clusters of five. The small, bushy shrub has dark green leaves, up to 2½ inches long, that develop a bronze color in winter. The plant works well in a mass planting and is frequently planted in front of larger shrubs. Low, hardy to –15° F. Blooms E–M. See Map 2.

**GINNY GEE:** 'Ginny Gee', one of the best rhododendrons, has tightly compact, twiggy growth. Broad, light pink flowers with white stripes completely cover the plant. It is very easy to grow. Low, hardy to –15° F. Blooms E–M. See Map 2.

**MARY FLEMING:** This delightfully colored Nearing hybrid is a recipient of the Award of Excellence. The early-blooming flowers are pale orange-yellow streaked with pink. The blooms are 1¼ inches wide and borne in small trusses. The early flowers can be discolored by a late frost. The leaves, 1½ inches long, turn reddish brown in winter. Low, hardy to –15° F. Blooms E. See Map 2.

The American Rhododendron Society
11 Pinecrest Drive
Fortune, CA 95540
707-725-3043
www.rhododendron.org

## SOURCES

You may not find every rhododendron, azalea, or camellia cultivar in this book every year at every nursery. While some have widespread distribution, other cultivars are available only when stocks are plentiful or through small, regional nurseries.

If you cannot locate a particular cultivar, contact one of the following societies: The American Rhododendron Society, the Azalea Society of America, or the American Camellia Society. Not only can they help you locate a source for the plant, but members often share seeds and cuttings of their favorite plants.

'P.J.M.'

**OLGA MEZITT:** With small leaves and clear phlox-pink flowers, this upright plant is well-branched if pruned when young; it is easy to grow. The leaves are bright green in summer and mahogany in winter. Medium, hardy to –15° F. Blooms E–M. See Map 2.

**P.J.M.:** The vivid purple-pink flowers of this popular, cold-hardy Mezitt hybrid are 1½ inches wide. Blooms appear early in small clusters. Dark green leaves up to 3½ inches long turn a reddish brown in winter. Growth and flowering are best in full sun. The plant is heat-tolerant, but in milder climates the plants often bloom in fall because they are stressed from the heat. Two varieties that are similar to P.J.M. but do not bloom in fall are 'Olga Mezitt' (medium pink) and 'Victor' (light purplish pink). Medium, hardy to –30° F. Blooms E. See Map 1.

**RAMAPO:** A hardy dwarf Nearing hybrid, 'Ramapo' has small, light purple flowers that appear early and may cover the entire plant. The 1-inch-long oval leaves are bluish green; new growth is dusky blue. It is excellent in a rock garden or as a border or edging plant. 'Ramapo' rarely grows taller than 2 feet. It remains especially compact when grown in sun, which it tolerates in cooler climates. Unfortunately, the plant is not reliably heat-tolerant. Dwarf, hardy to –25° F. Blooms E–M. See Map 2.

**SHAMROCK:** This exciting and unusual dwarf hybrid, which has 1½-inch-wide chartreuse flowers, gets its name from the fact that it blooms around St. Patrick's Day. It is a compact plant that grows wider than high;

leaves are 1¾ inches long and light green. 'Shamrock' looks striking planted in combination with other early dwarf purple hybrids. Dwarf, hardy to –5° F. Blooms E–M. See Map 3.

**WINDBEAM:** On this popular Nearing hybrid, the flowers are apricot-yellow in bud, open to pale pink, then change to almost white when fully open. Blooms are about 1 inch wide and appear early in the season. The growth habit is compact, and the 2½-inch-long dark leaves turn to a reddish brown in winter. 'Windbeam' tolerates heat well. Low, hardy to –25° F. Blooms E–M. See Map 1.

'Windbeam'

# RHODODENDRONS
*continued*

'Anah Kruschke'

# Elepidote Hybrids

Smooth, large leaves—4 to 8 inches or more in length—signal elepidote rhododendron hybrids. Blessed with an extended bloom period, some have a thick fuzz called indumentum on the undersides of the leaves.

**A. BEDFORD (SYN. 'ANNE BEDFORD' AND 'ARTHUR BEDFORD'):** A large, beautiful rhododendron, 'A. Bedford' is especially suitable as a background plant. Its slightly ruffled, 3-inch-wide, funnel-shaped flowers are pale to light purple, offset by a distinct dark purplish-red blotch. Up to 16 flowers may appear on the dome-shaped, compact trusses. Plants are vigorous with large, dark, glossy leaves about 6 inches long. Tall, hardy to –5° F. Blooms LM. See Map 2.

**ALBUM ELEGANS:** This old, cold-hardy Iron Clad hybrid has flowers that open as white tinged with light purple, then quickly fade to pure white as they become fully open. An attractive greenish-yellow blotch spots the flower throats. The flowers are about 2½ inches wide and are borne in tight, rounded trusses. The plant is vigorous, with a fairly open growth habit. 'Album Grandiflorum' is similar but has a slightly larger white flower with an olive-brown blotch. Tall, hardy to –20° F. Blooms L. See Map 1.

**AMERICA:** Another Iron Clad hybrid, 'America' has 1½-inch-wide, dark red flowers borne in tight, rounded trusses. Leaves are heavily veined, green, and 4 inches long. 'America' has an open habit, developing its best form in full sun. Low to medium, hardy to –20° F. Blooms LM. See Map 1.

**ANAH KRUSCHKE:** An attractive, compact, hardy plant, 'Anah Kruschke' tolerates sun and heat. Its light reddish-purple flowers are 3 inches wide and borne in cone-shaped trusses. The foliage is dense with dark green 5-inch-long leaves. Medium, hardy to –15° F. Blooms LM. See Map 2.

**ANNA H. HALL:** Expect disease and insect resistance from this attractive, densely foliaged, compact plant. White flowers arise from pink buds in ball-shaped trusses of about 15 flowers. New growth is conspicuously fuzzy. Low, hardy to –25° F. Blooms M. See Map 1.

**ANNA ROSE WHITNEY:** This lovely, popular Van Veen hybrid needs plenty of room and looks best in a large garden. Its funnel-shaped, deep pink flowers are 3 to 4 inches wide. The large, slightly open trusses may carry 12 or more flowers. 'Anna Rose Whitney' is a heat-tolerant and vigorous plant with attractive, dense, 6- to 8-inch-long, green foliage and an upright habit. Tall, hardy to –5° F. Blooms LM. See Map 2.

**AUTUMN GOLD:** The distinct, late-blooming flowers of this Van Veen hybrid are strong salmon-pink with an orange throat. They grow in trusses of 10 flowers. The shrub's foliage is dense; its light green leaves are 5 inches long. 'Autumn Gold' performs best in partial shade. Medium, hardy to –5° F. Blooms LM. See Map 2.

**BELLE HELLER:** The beautiful, pure white flowers of this Shammarello hybrid are 3 to 4 inches wide with a vivid yellow blotch on large, rounded trusses. A large, vigorous, sun-tolerant plant with good foliage, 'Belle Heller' often flowers in fall in warm climates. Medium, hardy to –10° F. Blooms M. See Map 2.

**BESSE HOWELLS:** This compact, medium-cold-hardy shrub with lustrous green foliage was introduced by Shammarello. The attractive, frilled red flowers, 2½ inches wide with dark red blotches, are borne in globular trusses. Plants occasionally bloom in fall in warm climates. Low, hardy to –20° F. Blooms E–M. See Map 1.

**BLUE PETER:** A popular Waterer hybrid, 'Blue Peter' has frilled, very light purple

'Blue Peter'

flowers with dark purple blotches. The plant is a vigorous grower with glossy, dense, green foliage. A reliable, cold-hardy, and heat-resistant plant, 'Blue Peter' is a favorite in the eastern United States. Medium, hardy to –20° F. Blooms M. See Map 2.

**BOB BOVEE:** This compact Bovee hybrid has pinkish flower buds that open to 3-inch-wide pale yellow blossoms with spotted red to greenish throats. Each truss bears 10 to 12 flowers. The leaves are 4 to 5 inches long. Medium, hardy to –10° F. Blooms M. See Map 2.

**BOULE DE NEIGE:** An old Iron Clad, 'Boule de Neige' is popular in the Northeast for its cold hardiness and rounded growth habit. The snowy white flowers are borne in tight trusses. The plant is heat-tolerant and can be used in full sun. 'Boule de Neige' is especially susceptible to lace bug. Where this insect is a problem, grow the plant in partial shade. Low to medium, hardy to –25° F. Blooms M. See Map 1.

**BOW BELLS:** L. de Rothschild introduced this beautiful plant. The contrast of the deep pink buds with the fully open, light pink, bell-shaped flowers creates a striking two-toned effect against the dark green foliage. New growth is reddish orange, adding to the colorful springtime display. A compact, rounded plant, 'Bow Bells' is best grown in partial shade. With time, it may reach 6 feet tall. Low, hardy to –5° F. Blooms E–M. See Map 2.

**BRAVO:** This attractive-foliaged Leach hybrid produces trusses of 11 or 12 light purplish-pink flowers that are lighter in the center with brown spotting. Tall, hardy to –25° F. Blooms E. See Map 1.

**BROWN EYES:** A dependable, large plant rated among the top five Dexter hybrids, this plant has good foliage and habit. Flowers are rosy pink with a prominent brown flare in a compact truss. Tall, hardy to –20° F. Blooms M. See Map 1.

**CALSAP:** This relatively new hybrid is outstanding, with a compact growth habit and good foliage. Pale purple flower buds open white with a dark reddish-purple blotch in conical trusses of 18 flowers. Medium, hardy to –25° F. Blooms LM. See Map 1.

**CAROLINE:** A hardy Gable hybrid,

'Bow Bells'

'Caroline' grows well in both hot and cold climates. It bears lightly scented, pale purplish-pink flowers on large trusses. The dark green leaves are 6 inches long with wavy margins. Medium, hardy to –20° F. Blooms LM. See Map 2.

**CATAWBIENSE ALBUM:** A vigorous, cold-hardy Iron Clad, this hybrid has flowers tinted pale purple in bud, opening to pure white with a spotted greenish blotch. The plant is covered with slightly convex, dark green, 6-inch-long leaves. Medium to tall, hardy to –25° F. Blooms LM. See Map 1.

'Catawbiense Album'

# RHODODENDRONS: ELEPIDOTE HYBRIDS
*continued*

**CENTENNIAL CELEBRATION:** Named by the Washington State Centennial Commission, this plant bears large trusses of 18 to 20 fragrant, ruffled, pink to pale orchid flowers. Leathery, deep green foliage clothes an upright, well-branched plant. Medium to low, hardy to −15° F. Blooms LM. See Map 2.

**CHIONOIDES:** This broad-spreading plant with attractive narrow foliage is sun- and drought-tolerant. Flowers are white with yellow centers in dome-shaped trusses. Medium to low, hardy to −10° F. Blooms LM. See Map 2.

**CHRISTMAS CHEER:** A hardy, medium-size plant. The pink buds fade to light pink flowers that bloom in March. Medium, hardy to −10° F. Blooms VE. See Map 2.

**CONNECTICUT YANKEE:** A new hybrid clothed in dark green foliage with a widely spreading, dense plant habit. Violet flowers with lavender throats are held in upright, conical trusses. Low, hardy to −25° F. Blooms M. See Map 1.

**COTTON CANDY:** This spectacular hybrid was developed for the Northwest. The pastel pink flowers fade to an even lighter pink. The flower buds are dark pink, and the contrast of the lighter open flowers against the darker buds results in an attractive, two-toned effect.

*'Christmas Cheer'*

The blooms, ranging from 4 to 5 inches wide, are carried on large, tall, upright trusses. It is a top-rated plant of vigorous growth with 6-inch-long, glossy, dark green leaves. Medium, hardy to 5° F. Blooms M. See Map 5.

**COUNTY OF YORK (SYN. 'CATALODE'):** A good, cold-hardy and heat-tolerant Gable hybrid. White flowers are 4 inches wide, have a conspicuous olive throat, and are carried in large, upright trusses. A vigorous, large plant with 8- to 11-inch-long, glossy, dark green leaves. Tall, hardy to −15° F. Blooms M. See Map 2.

**CREST:** One of the first good yellow rhododendrons, this hybrid was introduced by L. de Rothschild. The large, light yellow flowers are borne in large trusses. Young plants are slow to set flower buds, but once established they set buds freely. A vigorous plant with a habit of growth so open that many of the branches are exposed, 'Crest' replaces all of its leaves yearly. Despite some of its faults, it is still the standard by which newer yellow hybrids are evaluated. Tall, hardy to −5° F. Blooms M. See Map 3.

**CYNTHIA:** An old favorite, 'Cynthia' has large, rounded trusses with more than 200 deep pink flowers. The vigorous, upright plant tolerates heat and sun. In shade, its growth habit is open; in sun, it is more compact. Tall, hardy to −10° F. Blooms M. See Map 2.

**DAPHNOIDES:** An old variety, this plant is noted for its dense, glossy, rolled foliage, with leaves 4 inches long. The small, light purple flowers make tight, rounded trusses. This slow-growing, heat-resistant plant develops

*'Cynthia'*

'Elizabeth'

a compact habit. Low to medium, hardy to –10° F. Blooms LM. See Map 2.

**DEXTER'S APPLE BLOSSOM:** This vigorous Dexter hybrid produces large, six-lobed, fragrant flowers held in flat trusses. The 3-inch-wide white blossoms are edged with pink and spotted with a yellowish-green blotch. The foliage is dark green. Tall, hardy to –5° F. Blooms LM. See Map 3.

**DEXTER'S CREAM:** The fragrant flowers of this Dexter hybrid are pale yellowish white shaded with pink. These six-lobed blooms are 3½ inches wide and held in open trusses. Leaves are 3½ inches long. Low, hardy to 0° F. Blooms M. See Map 3.

**DEXTER'S ORANGE:** The seven-lobed flowers are pink with a brownish-orange blotch. The flowers are 3 inches wide and are held in open trusses of eight florets. The leaves are 4½ inches long. Low, hardy to 0° F. Blooms EM. See Map 3.

**DEXTER'S SPICE:** The fragrant blooms of 'Dexter's Spice' are white with a pale yellow-green spotted blotch. Each flower has seven lobes and is 5 inches wide. The leaves may reach 7 inches long. Medium, hardy to 0° F. Blooms LM. See Map 3.

**DEXTER'S SPRINGTIME:** This hybrid bears yellowish-white flowers edged in deep pink, with reddish-brown dots in the blotch. The blooms are fragrant, six-lobed, 3½ inches wide, and borne in flat trusses. Dwarf to low, hardy to 0° F. Blooms EM. See Map 3.

**EDITH BOSLEY:** An upright grower with dark green foliage, this new hybrid displays large, rich purple blooms with a darker purple blotch in the center. Medium, hardy to –15° F. Blooms M. See Map 2.

**ELIZABETH:** One of the finest compact dwarf rhododendrons, this hybrid is especially well-suited to the West. The large, bright red flowers are trumpet-shaped and often cover the entire plant. Each truss bears six to nine flowers. The plant blooms early and may be subject to some late frost damage. The dark green leaves range from 2½ to 3½ inches in length. Dwarf to low, hardy to 0° F. Blooms E–M. See Map 6.

**ENGLISH ROSEUM:** An old Iron Clad that is still popular in the East but seldom used in the West, 'English Roseum' is a good plant for beginners. Large trusses carry 1½-inch-wide rosy-lavender flowers. The shrub is vigorous, with smooth, glossy leaves. It tolerates heat and extreme humidity. Tall, hardy to –25° F. Blooms LM. See Map 1.

**EVENING GLOW:** A compact, medium-size plant with light green leaves, 'Evening Glow' has yellow flowers on very lax trusses. Hardy to –5° F. Blooms L. See Map 3.

**FAGGETTER'S FAVOURITE:** This plant is vigorous, yet it maintains a compact habit. For best performance, provide some shade. Deep pink buds open to a yellowish white tinged with pink; the throat is speckled with brown. The slightly fragrant flowers are 3½ inches wide and are borne in large trusses. Tall, hardy to 0° F. Blooms M. See Map 3.

**FANTASTICA:** An outstanding new hybrid from Germany, this plant has dark green foliage and an excellent compact plant habit; it is heat- and drought-tolerant. Flowers are a combination of near red and strong rose, shading to white in the center. Low, hardy to –10° F. Blooms LM. See Map 2.

'Fantastica'

# RHODODENDRONS: ELEPIDOTE HYBRIDS
continued

'Gigi'

**GIGI:** This popular Dexter hybrid has 3¼-inch-wide flowers that are deep pink with dark red spots. Each truss bears 18 blossoms. The glossy leaves are 4½ inches long. Medium, hardy to –5° F. Blooms LM. See Map 2.

**GOLDFORT:** On this cold-hardy yellow hybrid, pink buds open to 3-inch-wide, pale yellow flowers. The throat is a darker yellow with faint dots of green. Foliage is yellowish green. Medium, hardy to –10° F. Blooms M. See Map 2.

**GOMER WATERER:** An old Iron Clad, this hybrid is still popular in the East. The buds are pale pink opening to clear white with a faint green blotch. The late-blooming flowers are 3 inches wide and are carried in large trusses. This plant is tolerant of sun and heat, and it has attractive foliage. Medium to large, hardy to –15° F. Blooms LM. See Map 2.

**HALFDAN LEM:** An award-winning hybrid by Lem, this plant has 3½-inch-wide, bright red flowers marked with a darker blotch and borne in large, tight trusses. The deep green leaves are large, broad, and 8 inches long. The hybrid is excellent in the Northwest but mostly untried in the East. Medium to large, hardy to –5° F. Blooms M. See Map 5.

**HELLO DOLLY:** Another beautiful hybrid, this is a favorite in the Northwest. The 2¾-inch-wide flowers are two-toned and often called yellow, but they are actually a yellowish pink, blending to yellow in the throat with a few light green dots. The leaves are medium green with light beige indumentum on the undersides. Growth habit is rounded. Low, hardy to –10° F. Blooms E–M. See Map 5.

**HOLDEN:** This hardy, compact Shammarello hybrid is popular in the Midwest and Northeast. 'Holden' is heat-tolerant, but it flowers in fall in the Southeast. The deep pink flowers marked with red blotches are 2½ inches wide and borne in cone-shaped trusses. Leaves are a lustrous dark green and 4 inches long. Medium, hardy to –15° F. Blooms E–M. See Map 2.

**HOTEI:** The brilliant yellow flowers of 'Hotei' are broadly cup-shaped, 2½ inches wide, and carried in rounded trusses. The growth habit is compact. This plant requires good drainage. Medium, hardy to –5° F. Blooms M. See Map 2.

**JANET BLAIR:** The petals of this David Leach introduction (often incorrectly called 'John Wister') are pink and distinctly frilled; the blooms are 3½ inches wide. A broad plant with attractive foliage, 'Janet Blair' is vigorous and heat-tolerant. Tall, hardy to –15° F. Blooms LM. See Map 2.

'Hello Dolly'

'Janet Blair'

**JEAN MARIE DE MONTAGUE:** This beautiful old favorite from Holland is often listed as 'Jean Marie' and was originally registered as 'The Honorable Jean Marie de Montague'. The vivid scarlet flowers are in large trusses. The plant bears dark green foliage, and it tolerates sun and heat. Medium, hardy to about –10° F. Blooms M. See Map 2.

**KING OF SHRUBS:** The large apricot-yellow flowers of this plant are edged with a wide band of pink, and the 3-inch blooms are borne in open trusses. The narrow, pointed leaves are 2 inches wide and from 5 to 6 inches long. Medium, hardy to 0° F. Blooms LM. See Map 3.

**LEE'S DARK PURPLE:** This old, reliable hybrid is particularly suited to the Southwest. Its flowers are dark purple and bloom in fall in the Deep South. The plant is vigorous and heat-resistant, with wavy, dark green leaves. Tall, hardy to –15° F. Blooms LM. See Map 2.

**LEM'S CAMEO:** One of the few rhododendrons to receive the Superior Plant Award, 'Lem's Cameo' is particularly suited to the Northwest. But it may be hard to find because it is difficult to propagate. The 3- to 4-inch-wide flowers are light yellow suffused with pink. Each large-domed truss may carry up to 20 flowers. The new foliage has a reddish tint that changes to a glossy green. Medium, hardy to 5° F. Blooms M. See Map 5.

**LEM'S MONARCH:** A recipient of the Award of Excellence, this breathtakingly beautiful hybrid is a must for gardens in the Northwest. The 3- to 4-inch flowers are light pink edged with deep pink and borne in spectacular trusses. The plant is vigorous with large, dark green leaves. 'Pink Walloper' and 'Lem's Monarch' are considered the same plant. Tall, reported hardy to –5° F but tender in the East. Blooms M. See Map 5.

**LEM'S STORMCLOUD:** This plant has an upright growth habit. Its outstanding, upright trusses are tightly filled with glossy, deep red flowers that are paler in the center. Medium, hardy to –15° F. Blooms LM. See Map 2.

**MARDI GRAS:** 'Mardi Gras' has outstanding, dark green foliage with indumentum. Pale pink flowers fading to white with purplish-pink margins are held in ball-shaped trusses of 11 to 12 flowers. Low, hardy to –5° F. Blooms E–M. See Map 3.

'Lee's Dark Purple'

'Lem's Stormcloud'

# RHODODENDRONS: ELEPIDOTE HYBRIDS
*continued*

'Maricee'

'Noyo Brave'

**MARICEE:** A dwarf shrub with twiggy growth and shiny leaves, this plant has small, creamy white flowers held in miniature trusses. Dwarf, hardy to –5° F. Blooms M. See Map 3.

**MARS:** This old, reliable hybrid has deep red flowers with contrasting white stamens. It is a compact plant with waxy, ribbed, dark green leaves. 'Mars' grows best in partial shade protected from hot sun. Medium. Hardy to –10° F. Blooms LM. See Map 3.

**MISSION BELLS:** The pale pink flowers are bell-shaped, 2½ inches wide, slightly fragrant, and borne in open trusses. The plant is compact with small leaves. It is frequently grown in the West because it is sun-tolerant. Low, hardy to –5° F. Blooms M. See Map 3.

**MOLLY ANN:** Round leaves adorn a dense, compact plant with an upright yet dwarf growing habit. The rose-colored flowers have heavily textured petals, so they last well in lovely upright trusses. Low, hardy to –10° F. Blooms E–M. See Map 3.

**MRS. FURNIVAL:** This is a spectacular plant in flower. The light pink blooms have a distinct splashy red blotch and are borne in large, dome-shaped trusses. The shrub is vigorous, with attractive foliage and large leaves. It is a beautiful plant in western gardens and can be grown with protection in the East. Medium, hardy to –10° F. Blooms LM. See Map 3.

**NORMANDY:** Open, funnel-shaped, bright rose-pink flowers, which are deeper in color on the edges, adorn this low-growing shrub. The growth habit is broader than tall. Low, hardy to –20° F. Blooms M. See Map 1.

**NOVA ZEMBLA:** An old Iron Clad hybrid, this plant has 1½-inch-wide red flowers borne in tight trusses. A vigorous, tough plant, it is noted for its cold hardiness and heat tolerance. Medium, hardy to –25° F. Blooms M. See Map 1.

**NOYO BRAVE:** This hybrid has 2½-inch-wide pink flowers marked with a small red blotch. The rounded trusses may bear up to 22 flowers. Low, hardy to 5° F. Blooms E–M. See Map 3.

**NOYO CHIEF:** Recipient of the Award of Excellence, this hybrid bears 2½-inch-wide, ruffled, vivid red flowers on tight, compact trusses. It is a compact plant with excellent foliage. Glossy, ribbed, dark green leaves have a beautiful tan indumentum. This hybrid grows best in the Northwest. It is also known as 'Zeylanicum'. Medium, hardy to 10° F. Blooms M. See Map 5.

**ODEE WRIGHT:** This beautiful hybrid from the West Coast has 4½-inch-wide, vivid yellow flowers with a reddish throat borne in large trusses. Buds are a contrasting light reddish orange. A compact grower with wavy,

'Party Pink'

center, and the dark green leaves are blotched with yellow and occasionally have yellow margins. This shrub works well as an accent plant because of its interesting foliage. Growth is more compact in full sun, but in hot areas the yellow variegation can burn. Medium, hardy to 0° F. Blooms E–M. See Map 3.

**PURPLE SPLENDOUR:** A popular old hybrid, this plant has striking, dark flowers of deep purple marked with a black blotch. The growth habit is compact, and the leaves are dark green. Give this plant good drainage. Medium to large, hardy to –5° F. Blooms LM. See Map 3.

**ROSEUM ELEGANS:** A good, cold-hardy Iron Clad, the plant has 1½-inch-wide, deep purplish-pink flowers borne in large trusses. It is a vigorous shrub with medium green foliage. One of the easiest rhododendrons to grow, it is a good plant for beginners in the East and West. 'Roseum Superbum' is similar. Tall, hardy to –25° F. Blooms LM. See Map 1.

**SCARLET WONDER:** The vivid scarlet flowers of this aptly named hybrid are held in loose, open trusses. The foliage is glossy, textured, and dense. The growth habit is compact, and the plant tolerates sun well. Low, hardy to –15° F. Blooms M. See Map 3.

**SCINTILLATION:** One of the best known of the Dexter hybrids, 'Scintillation' received the Award of Excellence. The slightly fragrant flowers are pale to light pink with a distinct blotch of brownish-bronze dots. Blooms are 2½ inches wide and borne in large trusses of 12 to 15 flowers. This vigorous and sturdy plant is heat-tolerant and has dark, waxy, shiny foliage with leaves up to 6 inches long. Medium to tall, hardy to –15° F. Blooms M. See Map 2.

dark green leaves, this plant has seldom been evaluated in the East. Medium, hardy to –5° F. Blooms M. See Map 3.

**OLD COPPER:** A Van Veen hybrid bearing large copper-colored flowers in loose trusses, this medium-size plant has long, dark green leaves. Medium, hardy to –5° F. Blooms L. See Map 3.

**PARTY PINK:** One of the best new elepidotes, this Dr. David Leach hybrid has it all. Outstanding foliage, plant habit, and beautiful light pink flowers along with heat, sun, and drought tolerance make it a must for gardens. Its habit is upright. Medium, hardy to –20° F. Blooms M. See Map 1.

**PERCY WISEMAN:** This vigorous, compact plant's peach-pink flowers, which fade to creamy white with pale yellow centers, are accented by attractive, dark green leaves. Low, hardy to 5° F. Blooms M. See Map 3.

**PINK PEARL:** An old but well-known English hybrid, excellent in the Northwest, 'Pink Pearl' has large, soft pink flowers borne in good-size trusses. It is a vigorous plant with an open growth habit and light green foliage. Tall, reported hardy to –5° F in the Northwest but best used in protected sites. Blooms M. See Map 5.

**POINT DEFIANCE:** A spectacular hybrid, this plant has 4½-inch-wide white flowers with a beautiful deep pink margin that becomes lighter toward the center. The plant grows best in northwestern gardens. Medium to tall, hardy to –5° F. Blooms E–M. See Map 5.

**PRESIDENT ROOSEVELT:** This striking plant shows variegation in both flowers and foliage. The frilly, cherry red flowers have a white

'Scintillation'

## RHODODENDRONS: ELEPIDOTE HYBRIDS
*continued*

**SHAM'S JULIET:** Another cold-hardy Shammarello introduction, this hybrid has light pink flowers edged with a darker shade of pink and marked with brownish dots in the throat. The 2½-inch-wide flowers are borne in rounded trusses. The leaves are 3¼ to 4 inches long and dark green. Low to medium, hardy to –20° F. Blooms LM. See Map 1.

**TRUDE WEBSTER:** This Greer hybrid received a Superior Plant Award. The 5-inch-wide flowers are clear pink with faint reddish specks in the blotch. Dark green leaves grow to 7 inches in length and 3 inches in width. Although heat-tolerant, 'Trude Webster' grows best in partial shade. Medium to large, hardy to –10° F. Blooms M. See Map 2.

**VIRGINIA RICHARDS:** As the pink buds open on this beautiful Whitney hybrid, they

*'Virginia Richards'*

*'Trude Webster'*

fade to an even lighter pink, then change to a pale yellowish pink with a faint orange tint. The base of the throat is red with a blotch of reddish dots. The blooms are about 4½ inches wide. 'Virginia Richards' is a vigorous, compact grower with glossy, 4½-inch-long, dark green leaves. A word of caution: Not every shrub sold as 'Virginia Richards' produces the same bloom. Also, it is prone to mildew in humid regions. Low to medium, hardy to –5° F. Blooms M. See Map 3.

**VULCAN:** Fiery red, 2½-inch-wide flowers in heavy, domelike trusses characterize this compact shrub. It features dark, glossy foliage and is heat-tolerant. Several forms of 'Vulcan' are available, including 'Vulcan Flame'. Medium, hardy to –10° F. Blooms LM. See Map 2.

**WHEATLEY:** Popular in the East, this Dexter hybrid has fragrant, fluorescent pink flowers outlined by a margin of deep pink and accented by a splash of yellow-green in the throat. Blooms are carried in large trusses containing as many as 16 blossoms. The sturdy, compact plant has dark green leaves up to 7 inches long. Medium to large, hardy to –10° F. Blooms M. See Map 2.

**WISSAHICKON:** Especially popular in the East, this Dexter hybrid features large trusses of deep pink blossoms that hold up well in the sun. The attractive, dark green foliage grows in an open habit. Medium to tall, hardy to –15° F. Blooms M. See Map 2.

**YAKU PRINCE:** This dwarf cultivar, introduced by Shammarello, takes its name from one of its parents, *R. yakushimanum*. The 2¼-inch-wide pink flowers sport a pale pink blotch flecked with reddish orange. Spherical trusses hold from 14 to 16 blooms. Hardy to –10° F. Blooms M. See Map 2.

# Vireya Rhododendrons

Recently coming into their own as ornamental plants, vireyas offer good foliage and color. They cannot tolerate frost and do best at mild temperatures (45° F and above). Flowers form at different times of the year on individual plants, and some plants are in flower for a large portion of the year. The following hybrids are generally available and easy to grow. For all, see Map 6.

**ARAVIR:** A floriferous, compact plant with handsome foliage, 'Aravir' produces elegant, frilly, fragrant, pure white flowers with red stamens.

**DR. HERMAN SLEUMER:** An old favorite with olive-green leaves, bushy habit, and moderate growth, this excellent plant has large, beautiful, fragrant flowers of deep pink with a creamy throat.

**ELIZABETH ANN SETON:** The shiny, dark green leaves on this compact, well-rounded plant complement its reddish flower buds which open to flared, tubular, pale pink flowers. It is easy to grow.

**FELICITAS:** Good foliage on a compact, mounding plant makes this vireya popular. Its long, tubular, fragrant white flowers are flushed with pink. 'Felicitas' works beautifully as a hanging basket plant.

**GEORGE BUDGEN:** Bicolor salmon-orange and yellow blooms cover this vigorous shrub for two months starting in October. It was named for the founder of the Berkeley Horticultural Nursery.

**HANSA BAY:** A prolific bloomer, 'Hansa Bay' grows tall and branches well. Its red-orange flowers fade to gold; petals curve back toward the stem.

**JOCK'S CAIRN:** A vigorous, handsome plant, 'Jock's Cairn' requires a large container. Its ornamental trusses produce tubular, funnel-shaped flowers, which are pinkish red with pink throats.

**SAINT VALENTINE:** This dwarf plant with small, shiny leaves has an excellent trailing growth habit, so it works well in hanging baskets. The small, bell-shaped, bright red flowers also tend to hang down.

**SILVER THIMBLES:** A trailing habit makes this beautiful, delicate plant perfect for hanging baskets. The leaves are small, shiny, and thickly textured, and the plant's small, ivory-white flowers are flushed purplish pink at the base.

**VALADIMIR BUKOWSKY:** This plant has a spreading habit with good foliage on its stiff branches. It works well as a hanging-basket plant. Large flowers are deep orange with a bright yellow throat.

'George Budgen'

'Saint Valentine'

RHODODENDRONS
*continued*

## Rhododendron Species

The following are just a few of the 500 to 900 rhododendron species available from local nurseries and from specialty mail-order sources.

R. fortunei

R. augustinii

**R. AUGUSTINII:** The flowers of this bushy shrub from China are often described as blue, but they actually vary from light to dark blue-purple. Its bell-shaped blossoms are 1½ to 2 inches wide; the narrow leaves are 2 to 3 inches long. Several seedlings and named clones with interesting flower color have been developed from this species, which grows well in the West but does not tolerate heat. Tall, hardy to –5° F. Blooms E–M. See Map 5.

**R. CAROLINIANUM:** A native American species from the East, Carolina rhododendron has pink, funnel-shaped flowers that are 1½ inches wide and appear in midseason. Some plants have white flowers instead. The growth habit is rounded and compact, and the lepidote leaves range in length from 3 to 4 inches. Plants grow in sun and do well on the East and West Coasts, but they cannot tolerate the heat of the Deep South. Medium, hardy to –25° F. Blooms M. See Map 1.

**R. CATAWBIENSE:** This native of eastern North America has cup-shaped, 2½-inch-wide purplish-red flowers borne in large trusses. The growth habit varies from compact to upright spreading. It is cold-hardy but does not tolerate heat reliably. Several white forms are available, such as 'Catalgla'. Medium to tall, hardy to –25° F. Blooms LM. See Map 1.

**R. FORTUNEI:** This is one of the finest of the rhododendrons from China. The fragrant flowers are white to pale pink, 3 to 4 inches wide, and borne in large trusses. R. fortunei is a vigorous, large-growing plant with an upright, open habit. The foliage (dark green, 6 to 8 inches long) is attractive and rarely troubled by pests. The plant is often too large for the small garden, but it is excellent where a large, beautiful plant is needed. It is one of the parents, along with *R. decorum*, used in developing the Dexter and other hybrids. Tall, hardy to –15° F. Blooms E–M. See Map 2.

**R. KEISKEI:** Several forms of this species from Japan exist. The dwarf and compact forms are desirable. The small, pale yellow flowers appear early. Blooms are 1½ inches wide and are borne in small trusses. The lepidote leaves are 2 to 3 inches long, and the new growth may be bronze-brown. 'Cordifolia' and 'Yaku Fairy' are dwarf, compact cultivars of this species. Both are excellent for rock gardens or as edging or border plants. Dwarf to low, hardy to –5° F. Blooms E. See Map 3.

**R. MAXIMUM:** Native to eastern North America, this large plant has pinkish flower buds opening to shades of white, pink, or rose.

Blooms are 1½ inches wide and appear late in the season after the new growth develops. The plant is heat-tolerant and has an open, upright growth habit. It is commonly used as a background plant in the East. Tall, hardy to –25° F. Blooms L. See Map 1.

**R. MINUS (CHAPMANII):** These two species are often classified by botanists as varieties of the Carolina rhododendron. Both have pink flowers and lepidote leaves. Both are more heat-tolerant than *R. carolinianum*, and they are more open in their habit of growth. Medium, hardy to –15° F. Blooms M. See Map 2.

**R. MOUPINENSE:** A beautiful, early-flowering species native to China, this plant has fragrant, funnel-shaped, 2-inch-wide flowers that vary from white to pale pink with rose-purple spots. The lepidote leaves are 1½ inches long, and new growth is a bright bronze-red. Growth habit is open and spreading. It is an excellent plant for the West. Its flowers need protection from frost. Low, hardy to 0° F. Blooms E. See Map 5.

**R. MUCRONULATUM:** A deciduous species native to China and Korea, this is often called an azalea but is classified as a rhododendron because of the small scales on the undersides of the leaves. The 1¾-inch-wide purplish-pink flowers appear along the sides of the stems before the leaves emerge. Because the blooms appear so early, they are susceptible to damage by late frost. Leaves are lance-shaped and 4 inches long, and the plant's growth habit is open and upright. Heavy shearing increases the amount of bloom and the plant's compactness. This species often blooms at the same time as forsythia, making a striking color combination. 'Cornell Pink' is a clear, light pink selection. Medium, hardy to –25° F. Blooms VE. See Map 1.

**R. RACEMOSUM:** An attractive plant from China, *R. racemosum* blooms in early spring. Its small, white to pink flowers are 1 inch wide and appear along the branches and in small clusters at the stem tips. Leaves are 1 inch to 2 inches long, lepidote, and blue-green. Cultivars vary in growth habit and flower color. This species is frequently used in hybridizing. Low to medium, hardy to –5° F. Blooms E. See Map 3.

R. yakushimanum

**R. YAKUSHIMANUM:** This low, compact plant from Yakushima Island, off Japan, is considered one of the best species. The bell-shaped flowers are pink in bud, open to white or pale pink, and are 1¾ inches wide. The new leaves are covered with a soft whitish down. Tan to brown indumentum clothes the lower leaf surfaces. As the small leaves mature to their full size (3 to 4 inches), the whitish down is lost on the top of the leaf. The growth habit is rounded and compact. The plant is cold-hardy but does not tolerate heat. A popular species, *R. yakushimanum* is the parent of many new hybrids. Dwarf to low, hardy to –20° F. Blooms E–M. See Map 2.

R. catawbiense

# AZALEAS

| HEIGHTS |
| --- |
| **DWARF** |
| Under 2 feet |
| **LOW** |
| 2 to 4 feet |
| **MEDIUM** |
| 4 to 6 feet |
| **TALL** |
| Over 6 feet |

| WHAT THE BLOOM TIMES MEAN |
| --- |
| **EARLY** |
| Late March to early April |
| **MIDSEASON** |
| Late April to late May |
| **LATE** |
| June to July |

Azalea Society of America
Membership Chairman
P.O. Box 34536
West Bethesda, MD 20827-0536

Azaleas explode with color, their flowers blooming in a variety of shapes among small- to medium-size leaves. They are divided into four major sections: evergreen hybrids, evergreen species, deciduous hybrids, and deciduous species.

Azalea sizes are categorized as dwarf, low, medium, or tall (see left). Bloom seasons (see left) can vary by a month or more, depending on the climate. For example, in areas with mild weather, early-blooming plants may begin flowering by the end of February. In cold climates, the same plants bloom much later.

'Redwings'

## Evergreen Hybrids

The leaves of these evergreen hybrids change with the seasons but provide year-round backup for the drama of the flowers.

**BELGIAN INDIAN AND RUTHERFORD HYBRIDS:** The Belgian Indian hybrids and their American equivalent, the Rutherford hybrids, have tremendous variations in size, flower color, and hardiness. They shine as garden and container plants in warm climates; in cool climates, they grow only as seasonal container plants. The Belgian Indian hybrids can reach up to 10 feet tall and are hardy in Zones 8a to 10a. Rutherford hybrids are hardy in Zone 9 and reach 6 to 8 feet. See Map 4.

■ **ALBERT AND ELIZABETH:** The 3¾-inch-wide white blossoms have a green throat and are edged in deep pink. A standard greenhouse forcing plant, it also does well as a garden azalea in mild climates where it blooms early. Hardy to 15° F with protection.

■ **CALIFORNIA SUNSET:** This Southern California favorite has red early flowers, 2½ inches wide, with a pale pink to white margin. Hardy to about 15° F.

■ **DOROTHY GISH:** A Rutherford hybrid that is popular for forcing, this plant is exceptionally cold-tolerant. Hose-in-hose blooms are 2½ inches wide and appear early midseason. The frilled flowers are a strong reddish orange with a dark blotch. The sport 'White Gish' has snow white flowers. Hardy to 10° F.

■ **MADONNA:** A Brooks hybrid developed for florists, 'Madonna' is now commonly grown in western gardens. It features beautiful semidouble, ruffled, 3-inch-wide, white flowers in midseason. Hardy to 10° F (possibly colder with protection).

■ **NUCCIO'S TICKLED PINK:** A beautiful sport of 'Purity' that is available in the West, this plant has hose-in-hose, 2½-inch-wide, light pink flowers that are edged with white. Other Belgian Nuccio hybrids available in the West include 'Nuccio's Garden Party', featuring semidouble, deep pink flowers; 'Nuccio's Masterpiece', with large, double, white flowers with ruffled petals; and 'Nuccio's Pink Bubbles', with double, ruffled, light pink blossoms. 'Nuccio's Wild Cherry' has vivid red flowers. Most are early bloomers. Hardy to about 15° F.

■ **REDWINGS:** This popular Brooks hybrid, sometimes sold as 'Red Ruffles' or 'Red Bird', has ruffled, hose-in-hose, vivid red flowers that are 2¾ inches wide in early midseason. It is a good garden and forcing azalea. Hardy to 5° F.

■ **STARLIGHT:** A standard in the West, this Kerrigan hybrid makes a striking tub specimen. The semidouble, 3-inch blooms are a soft pink and yellow. Hardy to 10° F (possibly lower with protection).

**SOUTHERN INDIAN, OR INDICA, HYBRIDS:** The Southern Indian hybrids (sometimes known as Southern Indicas) are generally large plants with large flowers. They are more tolerant of hot sun than the Belgian Indians and are not tolerant of temperatures below 10° F. They can reach 8 to 10 feet in height. For most, see Map 4.

■ **DELAWARE VALLEY WHITE:** A white seedling of 'Indica Alba', this large, spreading plant is popular. Its early to midseason flowers are pure white and up to 2½ inches across. Hardy to 5° F. See Map 3.

■ **FORMOSA:** An older variety, 'Formosa' is a favorite in the South. Flowers are a deep purple-red with a darker blotch. Blooms are 3 inches wide and appear in early midseason. They blend well with white and pink azaleas but tend to clash with red or orange varieties. The plant is tall and upright. Hardy to 10° F (often sold outside its hardiness range).

'Koromo Shikibu'

'George L. Taber'

■ **GEORGE L. TABER:** This popular, cold-tolerant selection blooms midseason. It has white to very pale pink, 3½-inch-wide flowers with a light purple-pink flush and a darker blotch. Hardy, for short periods, to 0° F. See Map 3.

■ **GULFRAY:** A reddish-pink variety with a cascading habit, 'Gulfray' lends itself to hanging baskets and tall containers. In the ground, its prostrate habit keeps it low-growing, which makes it useful for foundation plantings. 'Gulfray' grows vigorously and flowers profusely. Discovered in a Mississippi garden, it was released in 1992, so it may be hard to find until nursery stocks are built up. Hardy to about 10° F.

■ **KOROMO SHIKIBU:** The early to midseason flowers are distinctive on this old

variety from Japan. The straplike, purple-pink petals are ½ inch wide by 1½ inches long and separated to the base. Koromo Shikibu is often listed as a Kurume. Hardy to –5° F. See Map 3.

■ **'LEDIFOLIA ALBA':** 'Ledifolia Alba' is an old variety found in Japanese gardens more than 300 years ago. It is often listed as a species (*R. indicum album*) although it has never been found in the wild. It is a large shrub bearing lightly fragrant, single white flowers accented with pale yellow-green dots. Hardy to 0° F. See Map 3.

■ **MRS. G. G. GERBING:** Popular in the Deep South, this early-blooming, beautiful white sport of 'George L. Taber' is not as cold-tolerant as its progenitor. Hardy to about 10° F.

■ **PRIDE OF MOBILE (SYN. 'ELEGANS SUPERBA', 'WATERMELON PINK'):** Popular in the Deep South and in California, this upright variety has deep purple-pink flowers with a darker blotch. The 2½-inch blooms appear in early midseason. Hardy to 10° F.

**KURUME HYBRIDS:** Profuse bloomers of small flowers in a variety of colors, Kurume hybrids grow to dense, shapely plants that do well as mass plantings. They are hardier than Southern Indians, to Zone 6, and all bloom in early spring. See Map 3.

## AZALEAS: EVERGREEN HYBRIDS
*continued*

'Blaauw's Pink'

■ **BLAAUW'S PINK (SYN. 'GLORY'):** Often sold as 'Glory' as well as 'Blaauw's Pink', this azalea blooms early to midseason. The hose-in-hose flowers are yellow-pink with a darker blotch and 1¼ inches wide. The shrub has a compact growth habit.

■ **BRIDESMAID:** The single flowers on this compact midseason bloomer, an old Domoto hybrid, are yellowish pink and 1½ inches wide. They have prominent stamens, and their soft color blends well with that of most other azaleas.

■ **CHRISTMAS CHEER:** Introduced by Domoto with the Japanese name 'Ima Shojo', this popular Wilson's Fifty has small, intense red, hose-in-hose flowers that are 1¼ inches wide. This early bloomer is dense and upright, often up to 7 feet in height.

■ **CORAL BELLS:** The Japanese name of this popular plant is 'Kirin'. It also goes by 'Daybreak' and 'Pink Beauty' in the nursery trade. The small, strong pink flowers are hose-in-hose and 1¼ inches wide. The growth habit is compact, and the early flowers are borne in profusion.

■ **HERSHEY'S RED:** An excellent azalea for the garden and for greenhouse forcing, this Kurume hybrid has strong red, early flowers that are hose-in-hose and 1½ inches wide. Other Hershey plants are 'Hershey Orange' and 'Hershey Cherry Blossom'. All Hershey azaleas are hardier than most Kurumes.

■ **HINO-CRIMSON:** This Kurume hybrid has small, vivid red flowers that hold their color well. It is a low to medium early bloomer with red winter foliage.

■ **HINODE GIRI:** One of the best-known Kurumes, 'Hinode Giri' has vivid purple-red flowers, which are best used in mass with pink or white azaleas. Avoid planting 'Hinode Giri' with reddish-orange azaleas—the two tints clash. Many named sports and hybrids from this cultivar are available.

■ **MOTHER'S DAY:** The flowers of this variety are vivid red with faint brown spotting in the blotch. Blooms are hose-in-hose to semidouble and 2 inches wide. The growth habit is compact, with red foliage in winter.

'Hershey's Red'

*In front:*
*'Hino-Crimson'*

■ **NUCCIO'S JEWEL BOX:** Intense pink, 1½-inch, hose-in-hose flowers highlight this dwarf plant. It grows only 3 to 5 inches tall.

■ **PINK PEARL:** This fine pink Kurume is the parent of the old pink Kurumes found in Japan. Its hose-in-hose flowers are an intense pink with a lighter pink center. They are 1¼ inches wide.

■ **RUTH MAY:** From a distance the flowers appear solid pink, but they actually have white stripes and a lighter margin.

■ **SHERWOOD RED:** This is a popular old Kurume with ¾-inch-wide, vivid red flowers on upright, compact plants. It is a prolific bloomer.

■ **SNOW:** This popular white azalea, introduced by Domoto Nursery, has hose-in-hose flowers that are 1½ inches wide and pure white with a light yellow blotch. The spent flowers often persist on the plant and are distracting.

■ **TRADITION:** A standard in the trade, 'Tradition' blooms in midseason. It is a medium grower with pink hose-in-hose blossoms.

■ **WARD'S RUBY:** The small, strong red flowers are 1¼ inches wide. They appear in profusion, covering the entire plant. One of the most tender Kurumes, it is easily damaged by cold even in the Northwest. See Map 4.

**KAEMPFERI HYBRIDS:** Tall and vigorous, these Dutch-raised hybrids often grow to 8 feet or more, making excellent background plantings or single specimens. Also known as Malvatica hybrids, they bloom in midspring (midseason) and are nearly deciduous in cold climates. Most kaempferi hybrids are hardy to Zone 5. For most, see Map 2.

■ **BETTY:** The vivid purple-pink flowers with a dark throat are 2 inches wide. The plant is a vigorous grower with a tall, upright habit suitable for training into a multitrunked tree-form shrub.

■ **CLEOPATRA:** The 2½-inch-wide flowers are an attractive deep yellow-pink. This tall, upright plant trains easily into a specimen with multiple trunks.

■ **NORMA:** The 2½-inch-wide flowers are an intense reddish purple with a lighter throat. This upright plant of medium height can be used as a multitrunked specimen.

■ **PALESTRINA (SYN. 'WILHELMINA VUYK'):** This upright plant has 2½-inch-wide white flowers with a light yellow-green blotch. Although very hardy, this plant can become deciduous during cold winters, losing most of its leaves; it replaces them in spring.

*'Pink Pearl'*

## AZALEAS: EVERGREEN HYBRIDS
*continued*

'Silver Sword'

■ **SILVER SWORD:** A sport of 'Girard's Rose', this new azalea has deep red flowers and variegated leaves with a narrow band of white along their margins. In fall, the leaves turn reddish with an attractive pink margin. See Map 3.

■ **VUYK'S SCARLET:** This old azalea from Holland has frilled, 2-inch-wide, deep red flowers on a compact plant. See Map 3.

**GABLE HYBRIDS:** The first group of hardy evergreen hybrids introduced in the United States, Gable hybrids take temperatures to −10° F; some can withstand even lower temperatures. Shrubs are low to medium in height, reaching 3 to 6 feet in 10 years. See Map 2.

■ **BIG JOE:** The flowers of this ever-popular Gable selection are a strong purplish-pink with a brownish blotch. Blooms are 2½ inches wide and appear in early midseason. It is a medium, spreading plant.

■ **CAROLINE GABLE:** Attractive, 1¾-inch-wide, vivid red flowers bloom in late midseason. This is a colorful, very hardy landscape plant.

■ **HERBERT:** The frilled, 1¾-inch-wide, hose-in-hose flowers are a vivid reddish purple with a darker blotch. Plants bloom in early midseason. They are low to medium with a spreading habit.

■ **JAMES GABLE:** The hose-in-hose flowers on this tall, upright plant are a deep pink with a darker blotch. They appear in early midseason.

■ **LORNA:** This plant is similar to Gable's 'Rosebud' but has larger rosy-pink, double, hose-in-hose flowers. It is a low-spreading shrub that blooms in late midseason.

■ **LOUISE GABLE:** The developer of 'Louise Gable' considered this one of his finest azaleas. The 2¼-inch-wide, semidouble flowers are deep yellowish pink with a darker blotch. The growth habit is low and dense. Plants bloom in midseason.

■ **PURPLE SPLENDOR:** The reddish-purple, hose-in-hose, frilled flowers of this popular variety are 1¾ inches wide and appear early to midseason. 'Purple Splendor' is frequently used in hybridizing.

■ **ROSE GREELEY:** One of Gable's long-range plans was to develop a hardy white azalea. 'Rose Greeley' was the result after 16 years. Its beautiful white, hose-in-hose flowers have a chartreuse blotch. The early, sweet-scented blossoms are 2½ inches wide. The plant is hardy and has a low, dense habit.

■ **ROSEBUD (SYN. 'GABLE'S ROSEBUD'):** The beautiful, double flowers on this hybrid open like rosebuds. Its 1¾-inch-wide flowers are a deep purple-pink. They bloom from midseason to late. The growth habit is low,

'Caroline Gable'

'Lorna'

Flowers have wavy petals and a heavy texture. The foliage is dark green and glossy.

■ **GIRARD'S JEREMIAH:** Large, pink, hose-in-hose flowers are backed by large, dark green leaves that turn red in winter. It is a medium to large grower and a prolific bloomer.

■ **GIRARD'S ROSE:** The early to midseason deep pink flowers with wavy petals are 2½ inches wide on this compact plant with reddish-brown winter foliage.

■ **GIRARD'S UNSURPASSABLE:** This broad, dense plant bears 2¾-inch-wide, deep pink flowers with wavy petals.

■ **GIRARD'S VARIEGATED GEM:** This new sport of 'Girard's Border Gem' has 1¼-inch-long elliptical leaves with an attractive yellowish margin. A neat, compact dwarf plant, it has deep pink flowers.

**LINWOOD HYBRIDS:** Developed in Linwood, New Jersey, for greenhouse forcing these hybrids have been improved to make good landscape plants that are hardy to –5° F. They have a low to medium growth habit. Spectacular colors characterize the hose-in-hose blossoms of these cultivars: 'Garden State Glow', with strong purplish-red flowers; 'Garden State Red', vivid purplish-red blooms; 'Garden State Salmon', intense reddish-orange flowers; 'Garden State Pink'; and 'Garden State White'. See Map 3.

dense, and spreading. It is considered the best of several different 'Rosebud' azaleas in the trade.

■ **STEWARTSTONIAN:** This attractive early-blooming plant has 2-inch-wide, brilliant red flowers. It is tall and upright with reddish-brown winter leaves.

**GIRARD HYBRIDS:** Hardy with compact growth as befits their Midwestern breeding roots, Girard hybrids display brilliant color. These low to medium shrubs reach 3 to 4 feet in 10 years. They are hardy to –15° F. See Map 2.

■ **CUSTOM WHITE:** The large white flowers are 2½ to 3 inches wide with wavy petals on a semi-upright plant.

■ **GIRARD'S BORDER GEM:** This sport of 'Girard's Rose' has early, attractive, deep pink 1½-inch-wide flowers. Its growth habit is dense, and the leaves are small.

■ **GIRARD'S CRIMSON:** A vigorous, compact azalea, 'Girard's Crimson' has large, glossy green leaves. Its crimson flowers reach up to 2½ inches in diameter. Plants are medium-size.

■ **GIRARD'S FUCHSIA:** This unusual azalea with beautiful early to midseason reddish-purple flowers attracts a lot of attention.

'Stewartstonian'

## AZALEAS: EVERGREEN HYBRIDS
*continued*

■ **OTHER LINWOOD HYBRIDS:** 'Linwood Blush' has light yellow-pink, double, hose-in-hose flowers. Those of 'Linwood Lustre' are white, hose-in-hose with greenish-yellow spots that blend into a dorsal blotch. 'Linwood Lavender' has light purple, semidouble blooms. 'Linwood Pink Giant' has strong purplish-red, hose-in-hose blossoms.

■ **HARDY GARDENIA:** Aptly named, this hardy plant has double white flowers and attractive dark green winter foliage. It blooms in late midseason.

■ **JANET RHEA:** This variety has unusually striking flowers for a hardy azalea. The hose-in-hose flowers are purple-red with irregular white margins. Blooms are 2½ inches wide. Hardy to –5° F.

■ **OPAL:** The double, deep pink flowers on this hybrid bloom in early fall as well as in spring.

**SHAMMARELLO HYBRIDS:** Ideally suited to cold climates, Shammarello hybrids are hardy to –15° F. They also are noted for their good growth habit. See Map 2.

■ **DESIREE:** This medium-size plant has 2½-inch-wide, frilled, white flowers. It blooms early midseason.

**'Ben Morrison'**

■ **ELSIE LEE:** A very hardy, upright plant, 'Elsie Lee' has semidouble, light reddish-purple flowers. It blooms midseason to late.

■ **HELEN CURTIS:** An upright grower with double white flowers, this plant is very cold-hardy. It blooms midseason to late.

■ **HINO-RED:** This is a compact plant with 1¾-inch-wide red flowers. There is no tint of purple in the blooms, which appear in early midseason.

**GLENN DALE HYBRIDS:** Originally produced as a large-flowering hardy hybrid for the Washington, D.C., area, Glenn Dale hybrids range from early- to late-flowering plants in a variety of colors. They reach 4 to 5 feet tall in 10 years. Still popular in the East, they are hardy to –5° to –10° F. See Map 2.

■ **AMBROSIA:** The deep yellow-pink flowers, which change to a light orange-yellow, are 1½ to 2 inches wide. 'Ambrosia' is an early-blooming, broad, upright plant; it grows to 8 feet.

■ **BEN MORRISON:** This popular, early-blooming hybrid of the Glenn Dale series was named in Morrison's honor after his death. The spectacular 2½-inch-wide flowers are deep yellowish pink with an irregular white margin and a purplish-red blotch. The white margins often do not become pronounced until the plant matures. A different hybrid with a similar name, 'B. Y. Morrison', has reddish-orange blossoms; its flower buds are not as hardy as those of 'Ben Morrison'.

■ **BOLDFACE:** The beautiful, white-centered flowers of this cultivar have a purplish-pink margin and a red blotch. The flowers are 3 inches wide and appear mid-season. This compact plant grows to 4 feet tall.

■ **BUCCANEER:** One of the best Glenn Dales, 'Buccaneer' has early-appearing, 2-inch-wide flowers that are a vivid reddish orange with a darker upper lobe. The flowers scorch in direct sun, so plants should be grown in partial shade.

■ **COPPERMAN:** The beautiful, deep yellow-pink flowers shaded with orange are accented by a dark blotch. The late-blooming flowers are 2¾ inches across, and the compact plants are of medium height.

*'Dayspring'*

■ **DAYSPRING:** The striking flowers of this top Glenn Dale azalea are 1½ to 2 inches wide. They have white centers shading to a light lavender margin. The broad, spreading plant is tall and blooms midseason.

■ **DELOS:** The 2½-inch-wide, double flowers are light purple-pink. Plants bloom midseason, and they are erect and spreading in habit. Flowers are heavy and may break the arching branches.

■ **DREAM:** This cultivar's 2¾-inch-wide, vivid purplish-pink frilled flowers are accented with a dark blotch. 'Dream' has an upright, spreading habit, and it blooms early.

■ **FASHION:** This tall, spreading early bloomer has 2-inch-wide, hose-in-hose flowers that are deep yellow-pink with a purplish-red blotch.

■ **FESTIVE:** The flowers of this tall early bloomer appear pale pink, but they are actually white with purple-red stripes and speckles. They are 2 to 2½ inches wide.

■ **GLACIER:** Another good Glenn Dale hybrid, 'Glacier' has early, 2½- to 3-inch-wide flowers that are white faintly tinged with green. Leaves are a dark, lustrous green and remain that way all winter. The upright spreading midseason bloomer is tall.

■ **GLAMOUR:** This is a beautiful, early-blooming azalea with 2- to 3-inch wide, vivid purplish-pink flowers. The plant is medium in height and spreading.

■ **HELEN CLOSE:** Beautiful, 2½-inch-wide white flowers with a pale yellow blotch in midseason characterize 'Helen Close'. It would be a good partner with 'Snow', 'Glacier', and 'Treasure' to make a long-blooming white azalea garden.

*'Dream'*

## AZALEAS: EVERGREEN HYBRIDS
*continued*

'Martha Hitchcock'

■ **MARTHA HITCHCOCK:** A real favorite, 'Martha Hitchcock' has beautiful white flowers that are edged in purplish red. Blooms are 3 inches wide, and they appear in early midseason. The medium, spreading plant occasionally produces shoots with solid purplish-red flowers. For an interesting effect, leave these on the plant until the blooms have faded, then prune them off.

■ **REFRAIN:** The 2-inch-wide, hose-in-hose flowers of this cultivar have interesting variations of white suffused with lavender, edged with white, and marked with pink stripes and a distinct blotch of purplish-pink dots. Some flowers show no white and are pale lavender-pink with a blotch. 'Refrain' is a tall, early-blooming plant.

■ **TREASURE:** This beautiful, near-white azalea is a good substitute for 'Indica Alba'. The pastel pink buds open to white with a very pale pink margin and pink dots in the blotch. Flowers are 3 to 4 inches wide. 'Treasure' is a tall, spreading plant.

**BACK ACRES HYBRIDS:** The large, substantial flowers of Back Acres hybrids tolerate heat well. Generally midseason bloomers, they are hardy to –5° F. The following plants are easier to find than the many cultivars available only from specialty azalea nurseries. See Map 3.

■ **DEBONAIRE:** The flowers of this variety offer beautiful, cool color for warm weather. The 3-inch-wide, vivid pink flowers with a light green center and a deep pink margin appear in late midseason. The plant grows slowly and remains low.

■ **ELISE NORFLEET:** Showy, pastel pink flowers edged in vivid red have darker dots in the blotch. The flower color varies on young plants.

■ **MARGARET DOUGLAS:** A popular azalea, 'Margaret Douglas' has spectacular, 3-inch-wide flowers that are light pink in the center and have a wide margin of yellowish pink. It is a medium, spreading plant.

■ **MARIAN LEE:** The 3-inch-wide, white flowers have a purple-tinged center and a red border.

■ **RED SLIPPER:** This popular midseason azalea has 3-inch-wide flowers that are a brilliant purplish red accented with carmine dots in the blotch.

'Refrain'

■ **WHITE JADE:** The 3-inch-wide, ruffled flowers are white flushed with pale green on the upper lobe. This azalea is effective with the stronger colors of the other Back Acre azaleas.

**ROBIN HILL HYBRIDS:** Late-blooming Robin Hill hybrids blanket landscapes with blooms in a variety of colors and flower types. Similar to Satsuki and Kurume azaleas, they grow between 3 and 5 feet in height. Most can tolerate temperatures to Zone –10° F. See Map 2.

■ **BETTY ANNE VOSS:** Buds open like a rose on this beautiful azalea. The double, hose-in-hose flowers are vivid to pale purplish pink and 3 inches wide. 'Betty Anne Voss' is a low, compact plant.

■ **CONVERSATION PIECE:** The 3½-inch-wide flowers on this azalea have wavy petals and are quite variable in color. Most flowers are white with a spotted blotch of purplish red, but some are marked with wedges of solid shades of purplish pink. Some of the colored flowers have a lighter margin. One plant may have the complete range of color patterns. This is a low, mounding shrub.

■ **DOROTHY HAYDEN:** This beautiful yellowish-white-flowering azalea has a low-growing, spreading habit. Each bloom has a green throat.

■ **LADY ROBIN:** A low to medium variety, 'Lady Robin' has interesting, 3-inch-wide, variable white flowers marked with wedges and stripes of vivid purplish red.

■ **MRS. EMIL HAGER:** This dwarf plant has semidouble to double, 2¾-inch-wide, hose-in-hose flowers. They're deep purple-pink.

■ **NANCY OF ROBIN HILL:** A low-growing azalea, this plant has semidouble to double, 3½-inch-wide flowers that are a light purple-pink with a light red blotch.

■ **OLGA NIBLETT:** An upright plant, 'Olga Niblett' grows as tall as 5 feet. Its creamy white, hose-in-hose flowers give a soft yellow appearance, unusual in evergreen azaleas.

■ **SARA HOLDEN:** This mounding plant has interesting, 2½-inch-wide, white flowers. The variable flowers often have five or six lobes to add interest to the color pattern.

■ **TURK'S CAP:** Aptly named 'Turk's Cap' has flower petals that curve downward in much the same way as the petals of a lily. Blooms are reddish and 3½ inches wide.

■ **WATCHET:** The ruffled, 3½-inch-wide flowers are a beautiful pink with a pale greenish-white throat. 'Watchet' reblooms in fall in the South.

■ **WEE WILLIE:** The 2½-inch-wide, light purple-pink flowers appear extra large on this dwarf azalea. It is a neat, compact plant.

**SATSUKI HYBRIDS:** For a profusion of late-season color, Satsuki hybrids make excellent landscape plants. Popular in bonsai plantings, they have a spreading, low growth habit and are hardy to about –5° F. More than 600 Satsukis are grown in the United States. See Map 3.

■ **BALSAMINIFLORUM:** A beautiful double form of *Rhododendron indicum*, this is a low, mounding plant. Its 1½-inch-wide blossoms are double, deep yellowish pink to reddish orange, and the petals open like a rosebud. An excellent specimen azalea, 'Balsaminiflorum' works well in front of larger shrubs.

■ **BUNKA (SYN. 'BUNKWA'):** The 4-inch-wide flowers have six rounded lobes. They may be white with pink flecks or a solid light to deep pink.

■ **EIKAN (SYN. 'EIKWAN'):** This variable azalea has large, rounded, 3- to 4-inch-wide flowers, often with six to nine lobes. The base color is white with many variations of stripes and solid colors of deep pink to deep yellowish pink. The plant is vigorous, spreading, and blooms in late midseason. The hybrid 'Linda R' has beautiful yellowish-pink blooms.

■ **FLAME CREEPER:** A low, creeping form of *Rhododendron indicum*, 'Flame Creeper' is excellent for trailing over walls, as a ground cover, or as a hanging basket plant. The 2-inch-wide flowers are reddish orange.

*'Olga Niblett'*

## AZALEAS: EVERGREEN HYBRIDS
*continued*

'Gumpo'

■ **GUMPO (SYN. 'GUNPO'):** The Gumpo group includes some of the best-known Satsukis in the United States. They are beautiful, low-mounding, late-blooming plants. 'Gumpo White' has 3-inch-wide white flowers with wavy, overlapping petals and occasional purple flecks. 'Gumpo Pink' flowers are pale to light pink with wavy petals. Those of 'Gumpo Fancy' are pink with a distinct white margin. 'Dwarf Gumpo' is a dwarf sport bearing 1½-inch-wide white flowers with pink stripes and flecks. 'Mini Gumpo' is a sport of 'Dwarf Gumpo', with 1¼-inch-wide white to pink flowers and ¼- to ⅜-inch-long leaves.

■ **KAZAN:** This compact plant has broad, glossy, dark green leaves, ½ inch or less in length. The leaves are often described as heart-shaped. The flowers are small for a

'Wakaebisu'

Satsuki, only 1½ to 2 inches wide. They are salmon-colored with a dotted blotch. This is a low, mounding plant.

■ **KEISETSU:** The attractive variegated leaves of this plant are dark green with small yellowish blotches and lines. The 3-inch-wide flowers are a strong red with a light pink to nearly white center. Occasionally, the margins of the blossoms are deep pink. The foliage provides an attractive contrast to the flowers.

■ **KINSAI:** The irregular flowers have separate, narrow, 1½- to 2-inch-long petals. The deep orange flowers seem spiderlike. This low, spreading plant with 1- to 1¼-inch-long, narrow leaves is popular for bonsai.

■ **MACRANTHA:** A selection of *R. indicum* often listed as *R. macrantha*, 'Macrantha' is a compact, mounding shrub of medium height with elliptical, 1½- to 2-inch-long, dark green leaves. The late-blooming flowers are reddish orange and 2½ inches wide. Other forms include 'Macrantha Pink', 'Macrantha Double', and 'Macrantha Dwarf'.

■ **SHINNYO NO TSUKI:** A spectacular variety, this plant has 3½-inch-wide flowers with overlapping lobes. The blooms may be solid colors or white with wedges or stripes of vivid purplish red or with a wide, purplish-red margin. This popular plant is the parent of many Satsuki hybrids.

■ **SHIRA-FUJI:** This beautiful midseason bloomer is noted for its variegated leaves. The flower color varies from solid purple to solid white. Occasionally, the flowers are white with stripes and blushes of purplish pink. It suffers leaf damage below 10° F.

■ **WAKAEBISU:** A popular landscape and container or bonsai plant, this hybrid has beautiful, 2- to 2½-inch-wide, hose-in-hose flowers that are deep yellowish pink with deep pink dots in the blotch. It is hardy to 5° F.

■ **WARAI JISHI:** An upright, mounding plant, 'Warai Jishi' has irregular double flowers that are 2½ inches wide and deep purple-pink with widely spaced, pointed lobes.

■ **YACHIYO RED:** This low, compact plant was introduced from Japan. Its colorful flowers are white with light pink blotches, stripes, or wedges. Sometimes the blossoms are solid shades of light pink. 'Yachiyo Red' is a good dwarf plant to grow in containers or in the landscape.

**PERICAT HYBRIDS:** Now hardy outdoors in many areas of the country, Pericats were developed for greenhouse forcing. Most of these hybrids are hardy to –5° to –10° F. The following are generally available. See Map 3.

■ **DAWN:** The flowers of this dense, spreading plant are 2½ inches wide, hose-in-hose, and purplish pink with a white to light pink center.

■ **HAMPTON BEAUTY:** The dark, candy-striped buds on this cultivar open to 2-inch, light pink blossoms. 'Hampton Beauty' is a medium, spreading plant that blooms in early to early midseason.

**NORTH TISBURY HYBRIDS:** North Tisbury hybrids excel as ground covers and look great in hanging baskets and trailing over walls. The dwarf, spreading plants are hardy to –5° to –10° F. See Map 3.

■ **ALEXANDER:** This late-blooming, low, creeping, irregular, mounding plant is usually less than 12 inches tall, except in the Deep South. The flowers are 2½ inches wide and deep red-orange with a dark blotch.

■ **HOT LINE:** A seedling of a dwarf 'Gumpo', 'Hot Line' has late-season flowers that are 3 inches wide and vivid purplish red with a deep red blotch.

■ **JEFF HILL:** The 2-inch-wide flowers of this low plant are deep pink with a red blotch. They have wavy petals.

■ **JOSEPH HILL:** This dwarf, creeping plant has 2¼-inch-wide, vivid red flowers with wavy petals late.

■ **LATE LOVE:** A dwarf, creeping plant, 'Late Love' has 2¼-inch-wide, bright pink flowers with a purplish-red blotch. Flowers appear very late.

■ **LIBBY:** This seedling of *R. kaempferi* has 1¾-inch-wide, light purple-pink flowers with wavy petals. The compact, upright plant blooms midseason.

■ **MICHAEL HILL:** A dwarf, spreading plant, 'Michael Hill' grows 18 inches high and 48 inches wide in 10 years. Late-blooming flowers are intense to medium pink with a purplish-red blotch. Blooms are 2¾ inches wide with frilled petals. 'Michael Hill' makes a good ground cover and is beautiful when allowed to trail down a wall. Hardy to –10° F.

■ **MOUNT SEVEN STAR:** A beautiful selection of *R. nakaharai* grown from seeds collected on Mount Seven Stars in Taiwan, this low, creeping plant remains less than 12 inches tall at maturity. The vivid red flowers are 2 inches wide with a faint blotch and wavy petals. This late bloomer is an excellent rock garden plant.

■ **PINK PANCAKE:** Less than 12 inches high, this low, creeping plant has wavy-petaled flowers that are bright pink with purplish-red dots in the blotch. It blooms late.

■ **WINTERGREEN:** This plant forms a circular mound, growing to about 12 inches high and 36 inches wide in 10 years. The deep pink flowers are 2 inches across. Plants blossom in mid- to late season.

**BELTSVILLE DWARFS:** Because of their size, these slow-growing plants are ideal for small gardens or borders, in containers, or as bonsai. Beltsvilles reach only 6 to 8 inches

'Hampton Beauty'

tall and are often as wide or wider than that. They are hardy to –10° F. See Map 3.

■ **BOUTONNIERE:** The 1½-inch-wide, hose-in-hose, white flowers have a pale yellow throat. Plants are dwarf and usually wider than high.

■ **FLOWER GIRL:** The dark pink, single flowers of 'Flower Girl' are 1½ inches wide and are borne profusely. Plants are twice as wide as they are tall.

■ **PINK ELF:** The light yellow-pink, hose-in-hose flowers are 1¼ inches wide and cover the plant completely. Plants are dwarf, about three times as wide as tall.

■ **PURPLE CUSHION:** The purple, single flowers are 1½ inches wide. These dwarf plants are usually twice as wide as tall.

■ **SALMON ELF:** The yellowish-pink, hose-in-hose flowers are 1¼ inches wide. A mature, 25-year-old plant grows less than 30 inches tall. Plants are usually as wide as they are tall.

■ **SNOWDROP:** The white, hose-in-hose flowers are 1¼ inches wide. Plants are usually three times as wide as tall.

■ **WHITE DOLL:** Single white flowers are 1¼ inches wide and cover the plant in spring. Plants are twice as wide as tall.

**GREENWOOD HYBRIDS:** Developed for the Northwest, these new hybrids range from low to medium in size. They are well-suited for both East and West. Hardy to 0° F. See Map 3.

■ **CAN CAN:** The frilled, purplish flowers are semidouble to double, 3 inches wide, and late. The plant is low, rounded, and compact.

■ **GENIE MAGIC:** This low, compact, broadly rounded plant blooms in early spring. The medium red, hose-in-hose flowers are 2 inches wide and cover the entire plant.

## AZALEAS: EVERGREEN HYBRIDS
*continued*

'Greenwood
Rosebud'

■ **GREENWOOD ROSEBUD:** This cultivar's roselike, 2¾-inch-wide, double hose-in-hose flowers are deep purple-pink. The plant has a low and compact habit.

■ **ORANGE SHERBET:** This low, spreading plant has double, 2¾-inch-wide, vivid red flowers in midseason.

■ **SILVER STREAK:** The leaves of this variegated sport of 'Deep Purple' have white margins and light mottling. The deep purple-red, hose-in-hose flowers are 2¼ inches wide. Plants bloom early.

■ **TINA:** The early-blooming, hose-in-hose flowers are 1 inch wide and a vivid purple-red. 'Tina' has a low, compact, and rounded habit.

**AUGUST KEHR HYBRIDS:** This small but select group of cultivars features excellent, double-flowering plants. August Kehr hybrids are low growers, but can reach 3 to 4 feet. They are hardy to –5° F. See Map 3.

■ **ANNA KEHR:** Each 1¾-inch-wide, lovely purple-pink flower has 40 wavy petals. The upright plant is quite compact. It blooms midseason.

■ **GREAT EXPECTATIONS:** A recent introduction, this low plant has red-orange, double flowers that are 2 inches wide. It blooms midseason.

■ **WHITE ROSEBUD:** The beautiful, 1¾- to 2-inch-wide, double flowers have 40 petals. They look like white rosebuds. Plants bloom early to midseason.

**HARRIS HYBRIDS:** A recent group to hit the United States, Harris hybrids have introduced more than 30 plants. They are low to medium growers, reaching 3 to 4 feet, and are hardy to –5° F. See Map 3.

■ **ELLIE HARRIS:** This hybrid has light pink, hose-in-hose flowers that are 2 inches wide and appear in early midseason. A low shrub (growing to 3 feet in 10 years), 'Ellie Harris' has a slightly spreading habit.

■ **FASCINATION:** The 4½-inch-wide flowers have a pale pink center with a red border. Flowers are fragrant, and their rounded petals create a starlike appearance in early midseason.

■ **PARFAIT:** The 2-inch-wide flowers are pink with a white center marked with a red-dotted blotch. Blooms are slightly fragrant and appear early midseason. The low to medium shrub has a rounded habit. See Map 4.

■ **PINK CASCADE:** This azalea has a cascading, spreading habit; it is excellent for hanging baskets or to grow as a late-blooming ground cover. The flowers are 2 inches wide and a deep yellow-pink with a red blotch.

**SCHROEDER HYBRIDS:** Attractive foliage combined with compact growth and cold hardiness add up to the versatile Schroeder hybrids. They reach 3 to 4 feet tall and are hardy to about –15° F. See Map 2.

■ **CARRIE AMANDA SCHROEDER:** The earliest bicolor to bloom, this medium-size azalea has a low, spreading habit. Flowers are single and white with a bright pink border.

■ **DR. H. R. SCHROEDER:** This low- to medium-growing plant keeps most of its winter foliage and has attractive pink flowers. It is hardy to –20° F. Plants bloom midseason.

■ **ELIZA HYATT:** This compact plant has light pink flowers with faint green spotting in the throat. Plants bloom midseason.

■ **MOBY DICK:** Early blooming and vigorous, this plant has large leaves and a low, spreading habit. Its flowers are large and pure white.

'White Rosebud'

# Evergreen Azalea Species

Native to Japan, most of the evergreen azalea species have adorned gardens for over 300 years. Having since branched out, many local and mail-order nurseries still offer these ornamental stalwarts for sale.

### *R. KAEMPFERI* (KAEMPFER OR TORCH AZALEA):
Good for mass plantings, this large shrub is usually evergreen but may become deciduous in cooler climates. Flowers range from yellowish pink to reddish orange. A rare white form also exists. Plants bloom mid- to late season. Hardy to –15° F. See Map 2.

### *R. KIUSIANUM* (KYUSHU AZALEA):
This dwarf species is from the mountains of Japan. The flowers are usually purplish pink, but a white form is frequently grown, and other colored selections are being introduced. 'Benichidori' is light reddish orange. The midseason bloomer is often deciduous in cooler areas. Hardy to –10° F. See Map 2.

### *R. LINEARIFOLIUM* (SPIDER AZALEA):
This unusual plant has narrow, straplike leaves that are 3 inches long and ½ inch wide. The flowers are violet and long and linear like the leaves. Spider azalea is of garden origin and has been known in Japan for over 300 years by the name 'Seigai'. It is a striking accent plant with attractive fall color that blooms early to midseason. Hardy to 5° F. See Map 3.

### *R. NAKAHARAI:*
Native to the mountains of Korea, this compact dwarf plant has deep pink to reddish-orange flowers that bloom late midseason. Hardy to –5° F. See Map 3.

### *R. × OBTUSUM* (OBTUSUM AZALEA):
Introduced from an old garden in China (the original plant came from Japan), this azalea has pink flowers. Obtusum azalea is no longer considered a species because it was not found in the wild. At one time, it was believed to be the parent of the Kurume hybrids. However, it has been determined that the original parent of the Kurumes is a rare species, *R. sataense*, from Kyushu Island off Japan. Hardy to –5° F. See Map 3.

### *R. SERPYLLIFOLIUM* (WILDTHYME AZALEA):
A low, dense, spreading plant native to Japan, this azalea makes a good bonsai subject. The pink flowers are ¾ inch wide, and the leaves are ¼ to ¾ inch long. A white form, *R. albiflorum*, is popular. The tiny flowers look like snowflakes on the plant in early spring. Hardy to –10° F. See Map 2.

**R. kaempferi**

# Deciduous Hybrids

'Gibraltar'

Gardeners throughout the United States can select from more than 500 deciduous azalea cultivars to fill nearly any landscape need. Most hybrids grow tall and are adapted to heat as well as cold. Most are hardy to between −15° and −25° F; some even tolerate temperatures to −35° F. For all, see Map 1.

**BERRYROSE:** The large, fragrant flowers of this Exbury hybrid are reddish orange flushed with pink and marked with a yellow blotch. The plant is a vigorous grower. New leaves start out with a reddish cast, then become uniformly green. Berryrose blooms in midseason.

**BRAZIL:** This midseason Exbury hybrid has frilled, reddish-orange flowers that are 1¾ inches wide and borne in large trusses.

'Brazil'

**CECILE:** This late midseason Exbury variety has deep pink flower buds opening to deep yellow-pink with a yellow blotch.

**COCCINEA SPECIOSA:** A Ghent hybrid, this is one of the best of the old varieties. Its late midseason, 2½-inch-wide flowers are reddish orange accented with a yellowish blotch.

**CRIMSON TIDE:** This new, large, mildew-resistant azalea, 'Crimson Tide' displays its large, double, red flowers well. It is one of the very best azaleas.

**DAVIESI:** Another old Ghent hybrid, late-blooming 'Daviesi' has fragrant, pale yellow fading to white flowers with a showy yellow blotch. The tall, upright plant is heat-tolerant.

**GIBRALTAR:** One of the best-known deciduous azaleas, this Exbury hybrid has frilled, 2½-inch-wide flowers that are a vivid orange tinged with red and borne in large trusses. Plants are heat-tolerant in warmer climates as long as they are well-watered and protected from hot afternoon sun. 'Gibraltar' blooms in midseason.

**GIRARD'S MOUNT SAINT HELENS:** This midseason bloomer's fragrant flowers are pink and yellow with a large reddish-orange blotch and wavy petals. Its growth habit is upright.

**GIRARD'S WEDDING BOUQUET:** Medium-size, with unique, apple-blossom-pink, hose-in-hose, frilled florets, this azalea produces as many as 18 to 25 fragrant florets per truss.

**GIRARD'S YELLOW POM POM:** Five-inch trusses of beautiful, double, fragrant, long-lasting, yellow flowers grace this compact, mildew-resistant plant.

**GOLDEN LIGHTS:** A mildew-resistant plant with fragrant, bright yellow flowers, 'Golden Lights' grows vigorously to 4 to 5 feet tall with an upright, spreading habit. It is one of several hybrids—the Northern Lights series—bred in Minnesota to tolerate extreme cold; all are hardy to −40° F. Like all Northern Lights hybrids, it is a midseason bloomer.

*'Golden Lights'*

**OXYDOL:** A fine white Exbury hybrid, 'Oxydol' blends well with yellow, pink, and orange-to-red azaleas. The 2½-inch-wide, white flowers with a distinctive yellow blotch appear midseason.

**PINK LIGHTS:** This Northern Lights hybrid has fragrant, pink flowers with orange spots in midseason.

**ROSY LIGHTS:** Another Northern Lights hybrid, this azalea has vivid purplish-red blossoms in midseason. It grows to 4 feet tall and will survive winters to –45° F.

**SATAN:** This medium-size, mildew-resistant Knap Hill hybrid produces vivid red flowers in midseason.

**STRAWBERRY ICE:** The midseason flowers of this choice Exbury hybrid are light yellow-pink tinged with orange and marked with a large yellow blotch.

**WHITE LIGHTS:** The midseason rose-colored buds of this Northern Lights hybrid open pale pink fading to white fragrant blossoms. Plants are hardy to –45° F and grow slowly to 3 to 4 feet tall.

**GRACIOSA:** An old Occidental hybrid developed in Holland, 'Graciosa' has fragrant, pale orange-yellow flowers accented with a yellowish blotch. Plants grow best in the West. It blooms in late midseason.

**HOMEBUSH:** Interesting, large, spherical trusses are a desirable feature of this Knap Hill azalea. The 1¼-inch-wide, deep pink, hose-in-hose flowers appear in late midseason. 'Homebush' is one of the most popular of the double-flowered azaleas.

**HOTSPUR:** A popular hybrid, 'Hotspur' has 4-inch-wide, reddish-orange flowers highlighted with a yellow blotch in midseason. The new foliage opens with a reddish tint. Hotspur has several named, sister seedlings, including 'Hotspur Orange', 'Hotspur Red', and 'Hotspur Yellow'.

**KATHLEEN:** This late midseason Exbury hybrid has beautiful, pale orange flowers blushed with pink and a deep orange blotch.

**KLONDYKE:** A superb late midseason Exbury hybrid, 'Klondyke' has flower buds that are reddish orange and yellow, opening to vivid yellow blossoms with a darker blotch. New leaves have a reddish tint.

**MARION MERRIMAN:** A popular Knap Hill hybrid, this plant has late midseason, wide, flattened flowers that are bright yellow flushed with orange and marked with a vivid orange blotch.

**NARCISSIFLORA:** The late midseason, pale yellow, hose-in-hose flowers of this old but still popular Ghent hybrid are a delight, and the plant's fragrance and heat tolerance are additional attractions.

*'Rosy Lights'*

# Deciduous Azalea Species

Native to Europe, Asia, and North America, species azaleas show off a rainbow of colors. The group includes some of the most widely available, frequently grown species.

R. calendulaceum

### R. ALABAMENSE (ALABAMA AZALEA):
This is a native of Alabama and Georgia. Its fragrant, 1½-inch-wide, white flowers have a showy yellow blotch. They appear in early midseason. A hybrid with pinkish flowers is often available as seedlings. Hardy to –15° F. See Map 2.

### R. ARBORESCENS (SWEET AZALEA):
Native to the Southeast, sweet azalea has 1½-inch-wide, fragrant, white flowers with contrasting red stamens. Flowers bloom in mid- to late season. Hardy to –15° F. See Map 1.

### R. ATLANTICUM (COASTAL AZALEA):
A native of the East Coast, this species bears 1½-inch-wide, white to pale pink, fragrant

flowers with a yellow blotch in midseason. It is a low to medium plant that spreads by stolons. Hardy to –15° F. See Map 2.

### R. AUSTRINUM (FLORIDA AZALEA):
This early-blooming species is native to the lower regions of the Southeast. Its 1½-inch-wide, fragrant, yellow flowers are often tinged with pink. Hardy to –10° F. See Map 2.

### R. CALENDULACEUM (FLAME AZALEA):
Native to the Appalachian Mountains, this species has 1¾- to 2½-inch-wide flowers that are yellow to reddish orange. There are two forms—one a midseason bloomer and the other a late bloomer. Hardy to –25° F. See Map 1.

### R. CANESCENS (FLORIDA PINXTERBLOOM AZALEA):
The most common native species of the Southeast, this plant has 1½-inch-wide, fragrant, white to light or medium pink flowers with a darker throat . Florida pinxterbloom is a medium to large early-blooming shrub. Hardy to –10° F. See Map 2.

### R. CUMBERLANDENSE (SYN. R. BAKERI):
*R. cumberlandense* is a variable shrub, usually ranging from 2 to 5 feet in

R. canescens

R. cumberlandense

R. schlippenbachii

Korea. Its early-blooming, fragrant flowers are light purplish pink to vivid pink and 2 to 4 inches wide. The leaves are 3 to 5 inches long, in whorls of five. This is a beautiful shrub when growing well, but it is fussy. For best performance, maintain a soil pH of 6.5 and supplement the soil with calcium. A white Royal azalea with a reddish-brown dotted throat is available. Hardy to –10° F. See Map 2.

height but sometimes growing taller. It is native to Kentucky, Tennessee, northern Georgia, Alabama, and North Carolina. Its flowers are 1½ inches wide, reddish orange to orange, and usually marked with an orange blotch. (The late midseason blooms appear two to four weeks after flame azalea.) Hardy to –20° F. See Map 1.

**R. FLAMMEUM (SYN. R. SPECIOSUM):** Native to Georgia and South Carolina, this species has flowers that range from yellowish orange to reddish orange and are marked with a large orange blotch. The shrub is low to tall and heat-tolerant. It blooms in early midseason. Hardy to –10° F. See Map 2.

**R. OCCIDENTALE (PACIFIC AZALEA):** This native of the Pacific Coast has 2½-inch-wide, fragrant flowers in midseason. They vary from white to pink to reddish and have a yellow blotch. Pacific azalea is difficult to grow in the East. Hardy to –10° F. See Map 5.

**R. PERICLYMENOIDES (SYN. R. NUDIFLORUM) (PINXTERBLOOM AZALEA):** The 1½-inch-wide, fragrant, white to pinkish flowers bloom midseason. A native to the East, this medium shrub spreads by stolons. Hardy to –15° F. See Map 1.

**R. PRINOPHYLLUM (SYN. R. ROSEUM) (ROSESHELL AZALEA):** This hardy plant is native to the Northeast. Its fragrant, 1½-inch-wide flowers are pale to deep pink; plants bloom in midseason. Hardy to –30° F. See Map 1.

**R. PRUNIFOLIUM (PLUM-LEAVED AZALEA):** Native to Georgia, this plant is valued for its late blooms in July and August. The flowers are reddish orange and 1½ inches wide. Hardy to –5° F. See Map 3.

**R. SCHLIPPENBACHII (ROYAL AZALEA):** The royal azalea is a tall shrub native to

**R. VASEYI (PINKSHELL AZALEA):** Native to only four mountainous counties in North Carolina at elevations above 3,500 feet, this species has 1½-inch-wide, fragrant, pink flowers with deeply divided petals. The early-blooming shrub is medium to large. 'White Find' is a good white selection. Hardy to –20° F. See Map 1.

**R. VISCOSUM (SWAMP AZALEA):** This species is native to eastern North America. The base of the fragrant, white flowers is a slender, 1- to 1½-inch-long tube, which terminates in short, 1- to 1¼-inch-wide lobes. The plant blooms midseason and spreads by stolons. Hardy to –20° F. See Map 1.

**R. YEDOENSE (YODOGAWA AZALEA):** This double-flowered garden form was discovered before the single-flowered variety R. yedoense poukhanense. The fragrant, 2-inch-wide, double, early flowers are light purple. It is a medium shrub that is semi-evergreen to deciduous in colder climates. Hardy to about –15° F. See Map 2.

**R. YEDOENSE POUKHANENSE (KOREAN AZALEA):** A medium-size, early-blooming shrub native to Korea, this azalea is often mistakenly listed as the species R. poukhanense. The single flowers are mildly fragrant, 1½ to 2 inches wide, and light to medium purple with a reddish blotch. Each blossom has 10 stamens. The plant is semideciduous, losing most of its leaves in colder climates. The Korean azalea has played an important role in the development of hardier evergreen azaleas in Europe and the United States. Hardy to about –15° F. See Map 1.

# CAMELLIAS

'Ave Maria'

With their sensual foliage and showy blooms, camellias reign today in beauty and longevity, just as they did in ancient China when they were revered by emperors and temple priests.

The American Camellia Society has developed six classifications for camellia flower forms: single, semidouble, anemone-form, peony-form, rose-form-double, and formal-double. See page 17 for photos.

Bloom seasons—which can vary by several weeks—are classified as early, before January 1; midseason, January 1 to March 1; and late, March 1 and later. Camellias planted in colder climates bloom later than those grown in warmer regions.

Most camellias grow into large shrubs unless stated otherwise.

American Camellia Society
100 Massee Lane
Fort Valley, GA 31030
912-967-2358

## Japonica Camellias

Most japonicas can endure occasional drops in temperature to near 0° F but will not survive long periods of freezing, windy weather. A few varieties can briefly tolerate temperatures as low as –5° F. Awards mentioned are from the American Camellia Society. For all japonica camellias, see Map 3.

**ADOLPHE AUDUSSON (SYN. 'ADOLPHE', 'AUDREY HOPFER'):** This award-winning, reliable, old French variety has large, dark red, semidouble flowers. It is a medium-size plant with a compact growth habit. Two sports are 'Adolphe Audusson Special', which has predominately white flowers, and a variegated form with dark red flowers spotted with white. Blooms midseason.

**ALBA PLENA:** One of the oldest camellias in cultivation, this popular award winner is mentioned in an early Chinese manuscript. Flowers are white, medium, and formal-double. The slow-growing plant has a bushy growth habit. Blooms early.

**ALISON LEIGH WOODROOF:** The small, semidouble flowers are pale pink turning to vivid pink at the edges. The plant has a vigorous, upright growth habit. Blooms in midseason.

**ARE-JISHI (SYN. 'ALOHA', 'BENI-ARE-JISHI', 'CALLIE'):** An old variety imported from Japan, this plant is appropriate for colder areas. The full-peony-form flowers are strong-to-medium red; the plant is vigorous, with an open, upright growth habit. A variegated form is available. Blooms early.

**AVE MARIA:** This popular modern camellia has small to medium, silvery pink, formal flowers. It grows slowly and has a compact habit. Blooms early.

**BERENICE BODDY:** This cold-hardy variety has medium, semidouble flowers of light pink, with the backs of the petals a darker pink. Plants grow vigorously and have an upright habit. Blooms midseason to late.

**BETTY SHEFFIELD:** A popular, award-winning camellia, this plant has medium to large, semidouble to loose-peony-form flowers that are white with red-to-pink stripes and blotches. It is a medium to large plant with a compact growth habit. It sports freely and has produced several well-known varieties. Blooms midseason.

**BETTY SHEFFIELD SUPREME:** The large, loose, informal-double flowers have a deep

'Betty Sheffield Supreme'

pink to rose-red border on each petal. The width of the colorful margin varies with each blossom. This camellia is a must for mild climates. It is an excellent plant for a cool greenhouse. Blooms midseason.

**BLACK TIE:** The small, dark red, formal-double flowers on this cultivar resemble a rosebud. It is a vigorous, upright plant. Blooms mid- to late season.

**BLOOD OF CHINA (SYN. 'VICTOR EMMANUEL', 'ALICE SLACK'):** The deep reddish-orange, slightly fragrant, medium flowers are semidouble to loose-peony-form. 'Blood of China' is an old standard variety that's still popular. Blooms late.

**BOB HOPE:** Large, semidouble flowers on this striking camellia are an intense dark red with purple-black markings on the buds and petals. Blooms midseason.

'Carter's Sunburst'

sport of 'Elegans' has large to very large, light pink flowers. Blooms early to midseason.

**DAIKAGURA:** An old standard variety developed in Japan, 'Daikagura' has medium to large, deep pink splotched with white, peony-form flowers. The slow-growing plant has a compact growth habit. The flowers are variable. Blooms early.

**DEBUTANTE:** An award-winning, vigorous, upright plant, 'Debutante' has full-peony-form flowers. The attractive, medium-size blooms are pastel pink. Blooms early to midseason.

**DR. TINSLEY:** The semidouble flowers on this cold-hardy variety start very pale pink and turn a deeper pink. The yellow stamens contrast and give the flowers a roselike appearance. The plant has a compact, upright habit. Blooms midseason.

**DONCKELARII:** The large, semidouble flowers of this standard variety are red marbled with white. This award winner has produced many named sports, such as the popular 'Ville de Nantes'. Blooms midseason.

'Bob Hope'

**CARTER'S SUNBURST:** Large to very large, pastel pink flowers have darker pink stripes and mottling. They are semidouble to peony-form to formal-double. Blooms early to late season.

**CHINA DOLL:** The medium to large, white flowers are blushed pale pink and edged with yellow-pink margins. The flowers have a loose, high-centered peony-form. 'China Doll' is a compact plant. Blooms midseason.

**CHRISTMAS BEAUTY:** The large, vivid red flowers are semidouble with fluted petals. The plant is vigorous and upright with pendulous branches. Blooms early.

**C. M. WILSON (SYN. 'GRACIE BURHARD', 'LUCILLE FERRELL'):** This

'Donckelarii'

**CAMELLIAS**
*continued*

**DRAMA GIRL:** An award winner, 'Drama Girl' has large, semidouble, deep yellow-pink flowers that appear on pendulous branches. The plant has a vigorous, open habit. It should be pruned annually. Blooms midseason.

**ELEANOR HAGOOD:** The pale pink, medium-size flowers are formal-double. The plant is especially good for cooler climates because it blooms late.

**ELEGANS (SYN. CHANDLERI ELEGANS'):** A well-known, award-winning camellia with large, anemone-form blossoms, 'Elegans' has deep pink flowers with white-spotted, pink, petal-like stamens. It is slow spreading and has produced many sports. Blooms early to midseason.

**ELEGANS CHAMPAGNE:** This sport of 'Elegans Splendor' has large, white anemone-form flowers with creamy white petaloid centers. The plant is bushy and spreading. Blooms early to midseason.

**ELEGANS SPLENDOR:** Flowers on this award winner are light pink edged with white. The margins of the petals and leaves are deeply toothed. Blooms early to midseason.

**ELEGANS SUPREME:** This sport has rose-pink flowers and petals with deeply toothed margins. It is compact with wavy leaves. Blooms early to midseason.

**FIRCONE VARIEGATED:** This award winner has tiny, deep red, semidouble flowers mottled with white. Blooms midseason.

**FLAME:** The large, semidouble flowers are deep red-orange with prominent yellow stamens. This vigorous, upright plant is a good cold-hardy variety. Blooms late.

**FLOWERWOOD:** A vigorous, compact sport of 'Mathotiana', 'Flowerwood' has flowers with fringed petals. Its large, formal to formal-double flowers are vivid red with a slight purplish cast. Blooms mid- to late season.

'Glen 40'

**GLEN 40:** Its large, deep red flowers are formal to rose-form-double. 'Glen 40' is slow-growing with a compact, upright habit. A variegated form, 'Glen 40 Var', is available. Blooms mid- to late season.

**GOVERNOR MOUTON (SYN. 'AUNT JETTY', 'ANGELICA'):** This old variety has a medium, reddish-orange, semidouble to loose-peony flower splotched with white. Plants are vigorous and upright. Blooms mid- to late season.

**GRACE ALBRITTON:** Award-winning 'Grace Albritton' has small, light pink, formal-double flowers edged in deep pink. Blooms midseason.

**GRAND SLAM:** This award winner has large, vivid red flowers with semidouble to anemone-form blooms. Plants are vigorous with an upright habit. Blooms midseason.

**GUILIO NUCCIO:** This award-winning, vigorous, upright camellia has very large, deep yellow-pink, semidouble flowers with irregular, wavy petals. Blooms midseason.

**HELEN BOWER:** The award-winning, large rose-form-double flowers are purplish red with white markings. Blooms mid- to late season.

**HERME (SYN. 'JORDAN'S PRIDE'):** This is a beautiful old variety from Japan, where it is called 'Hikaru Genji'. The semidouble, pink flowers are streaked with deep pink and irregularly edged in white. Blooms midseason.

**HIGH HAT:** This light pink sport of 'Daikagura' has large, peony-form flowers. It has a white sport, 'Conrad Hilton'. Blooms early.

**KEWPIE DOLL:** Its flower is a light pink, miniature anemone-form with a petaloid center. Blooms midseason.

**KING'S RANSOM:** The pastel pink flower becomes deep pink as it matures. Its form is loose with a petaloid center. Blooms midseason.

**KRAMER'S SUPREME:** Its large, vivid red, slightly fragrant, peony-form flower has a tint of orange. Growth is vigorous, dense, and upright. Blooms midseason.

**KUMASAKA:** An old Japanese variety, 'Kumasaka' has medium, rose-pink flowers that vary from rose-form-double to peony-form. Blooms mid- to late season.

**LADY CLARE (SYN. 'EMPRESS'):** The Japanese name for this award-winning, old variety is 'Akashigata'. Its large, deep pink flowers have prominent yellow stamens. 'Oniji' is a variegated sport. Blooms early midseason.

**LADY KAY:** A sport of 'Ville de Nantes', this award winner has large, red-blotched-white, loose- to full-peony, sometimes fringed, flowers. Blooms midseason.

**LADY VANSITTART:** This old but popular variety has medium, semidouble flowers with broad, wavy petals. Color varies but is usually white with a faint blush and light pink stripes. Slow growing and bushy, it is cold-hardy. Blooms mid- to late season.

**LITTLE SLAM:** This award-winning, red miniature has full-peony-form flowers. Blooms early to midseason.

**MAGNOLIAEFLORA:** An old but popular, award-winning variety, 'Magnoliaeflora' has pale pink flowers that are semidouble with prominent yellow stamens. Blooms midseason.

**MARGARET DAVIS:** This award-winning camellia has white to pale yellow-white full-peony-form flowers edged in a vivid red. Blooms midseason.

**MATHOTIANA:** This popular, award-winning old variety has large to very large rose-form to formal-double crimson flowers. A sport, 'Mathotiana Supreme', has large, semidouble, crimson flowers with yellow stamens. Flowers can be blotched with white. Blooms mid- to late season.

**MISS CHARLESTON:** The large, deep red, award-winning flowers are semidouble with a high center. A variegated form is available. Blooms midseason.

**MRS. D. W. DAVIS:** Large, pale pink, semidouble flowers with prominent, yellow, petal-like stamens highlight 'Mrs. D. W. Davis'. These prize-winning plants are dense and vigorous. Blooms midseason.

**MRS. TINGLEY:** This compact, cold-hardy plant has formal-double, yellow-pink flowers. Blooms mid- to late season.

**NUCCIO'S GEM:** A popular award winner, this camellia has white, formal-double flowers and vigorous growth with dense, glossy foliage. Blooms early to midseason.

**NUCCIO'S PEARL:** The beautiful, double, pale pink flowers are edged in a deeper pink. The compact plants are excellent container specimens. Blooms midseason.

**PINK PAGODA:** The large, deep pink, formal-double flowers have wavy petals. 'Pink Frost' is a pink sport with petals edged in white. Blooms early to midseason.

**PINK PERFECTION:** Known worldwide, this long-blooming, award-winner has small, shell pink, formal-double flowers. Blooms early to midseason.

**PROFESSOR CHARLES S. SARGENT:** This cold-hardy variety, called 'Christmas Carnation' in the South, has dark red, loose-peony-form flowers with an anemone center. There is a variegated sport. Blooms midseason.

**R. L. WHEELER:** Award-winning 'R. L. Wheeler' has large, deep pink, semidouble to anemone-form flowers with a solid center of stamens and upright vigorous growth. Blooms early to midseason.

**SAWADA'S DREAM:** The perfect formal-double flowers are white in the center with the outer third shaded a pale pink. Petals are pointed and well-formed. 'Sawada's Dream' is a recipient of the National Hall of Fame Award. Blooms midseason.

**SEA FOAM:** This camellia has large, white, formal-double flowers and an upright growth habit. Blooms late.

'Lady Clare'

**SEPTEMBER MORN (SYN. 'YOHEI HAKU'):** This early variety grows well in cool areas. The white to pale pink flowers vary from semidouble to peony-form to anemone-form. Blooms early.

**SILVER CHALICE:** One of the best whites, 'Silver Chalice' has large, full-peony-form flowers. The fluted, upright petals give a rounded effect. Blooms midseason.

**SNOWMAN:** This award-winning plant with large, white, semidouble flowers has an upright, spreading habit. Blooms midseason.

**TIFFANY:** The flowers of this award winner vary from loose to peony to anemone. Blooms are large and light purple-pink edged with deeper pink. Plants are vigorous with an upright habit. Blooms midseason.

**TOMORROW'S DAWN:** The flowers are pale pink, fading toward white edges. Flowers can have white petal-like stamens and red streaks. Blooms early to midseason.

**VILLE DE NANTES:** Old but still popular, 'Ville de Nantes' is an award-winning variety with medium to large, semidouble, fringed flowers. Its upright petals are dark red with white blotches. Blooms midseason to late.

**CAMELLIAS**
*continued*

# Sasanqua Camellias

Blooming profusely in the fall with bushy growth, sasanqua camellias make elegant hedges and foundation and screen plantings. They are hardy to 10° F.

**BETTIE PATRICIA:** A popular, light pink, rose-form-double sasanqua, 'Bettie Patricia' is upright and spreading. Blooms fall. See Map 3.

**BONANZA:** Award-winning 'Bonanza' has large, deep red, semidouble flowers and wavy, fluted petals. Blooms early fall. See Map 3.

'Bonanza'

**BONSAI BABY:** The small, deep red flowers of 'Bonsai Baby' are formal-double to rose-form-double. The plant is a compact cultivar of *C. hiemalis* and a favorite container and bonsai plant. Blooms fall. See Map 3.

**CHANSONETTE:** This award-winning *C. hiemalis* cultivar has large, pink, semidouble blooms with ruffled petals on a bushy plant. Blooms early. See Map 3.

**CLEOPATRA:** Light to deep pink, semi-double flowers and a bushy habit highlight 'Cleopatra'. It has two sports: 'Cleopatra Blush', pale pink, and 'Cleopatra White'. Blooms early to mid fall. See Map 3.

**COTTON CANDY:** This popular sasanqua has an upright, spreading habit and large, pink, semidouble flowers with ruffled petals. Blooms early fall. See Map 3.

**DAWN (SYN. 'GINRYU', 'GINRYO'):** A cultivar of *C. vernalis*, 'Dawn' has semidouble flowers that are white blushed with pink. The blossoms last a long time on the plant, so they are susceptible to damage by an early freeze. Blooms late fall. See Map 3.

**DAZZLER:** The deep pink to red flowers of this *C. hiemalis* cultivar are semidouble with wavy petals. 'Dazzler' is a vigorous plant with a spreading, upright habit. Blooms early fall. See Map 3.

**JEAN MAY:** This popular landscape plant and container specimen has large, pink, double flowers that provide a beautiful fall display. It is best used in partial shade because the flowers can fade in direct sun. Blooms fall. See Map 3.

**MINE-NO-YUKI (SYN. 'SNOW', 'SNOW ON THE MOUNTAIN', 'WHITE DOVE'):** A popular sasanqua, this bushy plant produces an abundance of semidouble, white flowers that literally cover the plant. It is an excellent landscape plant as well as a container specimen. Blooms late fall. See Map 3.

**NARUMI-GATA:** Vigorous, upright growth and large, white, single flowers shaded light pink are the hallmark of 'Narumi-Gata'. Its blooms are cup-shaped and have a crinkled texture. This cultivar is often called 'Oleifera', but it should not be confused with *C. oleifera*. Blooms midseason. See Map 3.

**OUR LINDA:** This sasanqua has excellent, pink, rose-form-double flowers and an upright, dense habit. Blooms early. See Map 3.

'Jean May'

*'Shishi
Gashira'*

**PINK SNOW:** The large, light pink, semi-double flowers of this bushy plant are faintly blushed with purple. Blooms late. See Map 3.

**SETSUGEKKA (SYN. 'ELEGANT FRIEND', 'FLUTED WHITE', 'WAVY WHITE'):** This favorite sasanqua has large, white, semidouble flowers with ruffled petals. The plant has a vigorous, upright habit and displays the flowers well. Blooms early to late. See Map 3.

**SHISHI GASHIRA (SYN. 'LION HEAD'):** A popular *C. hiemalis* cultivar, 'Shishi Gashira' has deep pink, semidouble to double flowers with fluted petals and a compact habit. Blooms late. See Map 3.

**SHOWA-NO-SAKAE (SYN. 'GLORY', 'USUBENI'):** This *C. hiemalis* cultivar has semidouble to rose-form-double, light pink flowers, sometimes marbled with white. It is a low-growing, compact camellia that does well as a landscaping plant, an espalier, or in containers. Blooms early fall. See Map 3.

**SPARKLING BURGUNDY:** Its excellent floral display has made 'Sparkling Burgundy' a popular sasanqua. The small, peony-form flowers are deep purple-pink with a light purple blush. It is a tall, upright, spreading plant. Blooms early. See Map 3.

**STAR ABOVE STAR:** An award-winning cultivar of *C. vernalis*, this plant has semi-double flowers that are white, changing to purplish pink at the edges. The petals are crinkled, and the flowers have a starlike appearance. Blooms late. See Map 3.

**TANYA:** This popular sasanqua was named for the title of a Japanese drama. The small, single flowers are deep pink with prominent yellow stamens. The plant is low, with small leaves and a bushy, spreading habit. It makes a good ground cover. Blooms early to midseason. See Map 3.

**YULETIDE:** An award-winning favorite, this sasanqua bears its small, single, reddish-orange flowers in profusion. Petals are broad and rounded, setting off the mass of yellow stamens nicely. 'Yuletide' is a compact plant, excellent for the landscape and as a container specimen. Blooms late fall. See Map 3.

*'Sparkling
Burgundy'*

CAMELLIAS
*continued*

'Shot Silk'

# Reticulata Camellias

Unlike other camellia species, the leaves of reticulatas have a matte, rather than glossy, finish; their flowers are large. They are hardy to only 25° F. For all reticulatas, see Map 4.

**'BUDDHA':** One of the early hybrids, this camellia was introduced from China. Its large, deep pink, semidouble flowers have upright, wavy petals. Blooms mid- to late season.

'Captain Rawes'

**CAPTAIN RAWES:** The very large, deep pink flowers are semidouble to loose-peony in form. The plant is vigorous and upright. Blooms late.

**CRIMSON ROBE (SYN. 'DATAOHONG'):** This award-winning cultivar has large, semidouble, red flowers with wavy, crinkled petals. The plant has a vigorous, spreading growth habit. Leaves are sometimes variegated with a yellowish-white margin. Blooms midseason.

**PAGODA:** Often called by its Chinese name, 'Songzlin', this reticulata from China has large, formal-double to rose-form-double flowers that are a deep reddish orange. Blooms midseason.

**SHOT SILK (SYN. 'DAYIUHONG'):** This beautiful introduction from China has very large, semidouble flowers of a striking vivid pink. The petals have wavy margins. Blooms early.

# Higo Camellias

Used in bonsai and containers in Japan, over 20 Higo camellia cultivars stud the American landscape. They are slightly hardier than japonicas, to Zone 7. For all Higos, see Map 3.

**ASAGAO:** The medium, single flowers are pale pink with flared stamens. The plant has a bushy habit. Blooms early to midseason.

**HI-NO-MARU:** The single, medium-size, red flowers have wavy petals. Growth is slow, upright, and compact. Blooms midseason.

**JITSU-GETSU-SE:** Single, medium-size flowers are red splotched with white and are flat with flared stamens. The plant is vigorous with an upright growth habit. Blooms mid- to late season.

**MANGETSU:** The single, medium, white flowers have golden, flared stamens. 'Mangetsu' is a vigorous, upright grower. Blooms midseason.

**TENJU:** The medium to large, single, blush pink flowers have flared stamens. This plant is a vigorous grower, with an open, upright habit. Blooms midseason.

# Other Camellia Hybrids

Breeding continues in the United States, Australia, New Zealand, Japan, China, England, and Europe for camellia hybrids. Hardiness of many of these cultivars is not known but is assumed to be similar to that of japonicas, which are hardy to near 0° F. The following list includes hybrid camellias with parents other than C. *reticulata*. See Map 3.

**ACK-SCENT:** The delightfully fragrant, peony-form flower is light pink. Blooms mid- to late season.

**ANGEL WINGS:** The semidouble flowers are white shaded with purplish pink, and the narrow, wavy petals are upright. Blooms midseason.

**ANTICIPATION:** This award-winning Williamsii hybrid has large, deep pink, peony-form flowers. A variegated sport is available. Blooms midseason.

**BABY BEAR:** The small, single flowers of this attractive, miniature camellia are light pink with occasional white blotches. It is a dwarf plant. Blooms midseason.

**CHARLEAN:** The beautiful, large, semidouble pink flowers with faint purplish overtones have pink stamens tipped with yellow. The award-winning plant is vigorous, with a spreading habit. Blooms mid- to late season.

**CHINA LADY:** This upright, medium-size plant has very large, semidouble flowers that are rich orchid-pink. The leaves are long, narrow, and beautifully veined. Blooms early midseason.

**DR. CLIFFORD PARKS:** This vigorous, upright-growing plant produces very large, rich red, anemone-form flowers. Blooms midseason.

**DONATION:** The large, light purple-pink flowers of this award-winning Williamsii are semidouble. It is a vigorous plant with dense,

upright growth. A variegated sport is available. Blooms midseason.

**FRANCIE L.:** Flowers on this plant are semidouble, rose-pink and very large, with irregular, upright, wavy petals. Blooms mid- to late season.

**JEAN PURSEL:** This vigorous, upright plant of open habit produces very large, light orchid-pink, peony-form flowers. Blooms mid- to late season.

**LASCA BEAUTY:** The large, semidouble blooms on this upright, compact plant are a rich, soft pink with heavy-textured petals. Blooms midseason.

**NUCCIO'S RUBY:** This plant's habit is upright and bushy. Its flowers are large, dark rich red, ruffled, and semidouble. Blooms midseason.

**VALENTINES DAY:** The formal-double flowers on this plant are very large and medium salmon-pink. It is a slow, upright grower. Blooms midseason.

'Anticipation'

# Camellia Species

The genus *Camellia* boasts over 200 species, but most are not available in the Western world. Those that are require warm climates, as many are less hardy than japonicas and sasanquas. The following are the more common and readily available species.

C. saluenensis

**C. CHRYSANTHA:** This rare, yellow species from China was introduced to the Western world in 1980 and bloomed for the first time during the 1984–85 season. Its small, single to semidouble, yellow flowers have shiny, heavily textured petals. The plant is vigorous, with an upright, open habit. This species has had limited availability for many years. Blooms midseason. See Map 4.

**C. CUSPIDATA:** Native to southern China, this species has small, single, white flowers and pointed leaves. Blooms midseason. See Map 4.

**C. FRATERNA:** The mildly fragrant, small, single flowers of this native of central China are white flushed with pale purple. The flowers grow in small clusters. The plant is a small shrub. Blooms midseason. See Map 4.

**C. GRANTHAMIANA:** The large, white flowers have clusters of prominent yellow stamens. Leaves are large, to 4 inches long, with wrinkled surfaces. The only known existing wild plant is a small tree in Hong Kong. Blooms early. See Map 4.

**C. JAPONICA:** This small tree—native to Japan, Korea, and eastern China—has deep pink to red flowers in the wild. It is best known in its many garden forms. Blooms early. See Map 3.

**C. LUTCHUENSIS:** The small, white flowers are very fragrant. Leaves are small and sharply pointed. This species is used in hybridizing for fragrance. Blooms midseason. See Map 4.

**C. MALIFLORA (SYN. 'BETTY MCCASKILL'):** Native to central China, this species has small, pink, semidouble flowers. Leaves are small and pointed. Blooms mid- to late season. See Map 4.

**C. OLEIFERA:** This species has fragrant, single, white flowers. Its growth habit is upright to semicascading. A native of China, it is cultivated there for its seed oil. Blooms midseason. See Map 3.

**C. ROSIFLORA:** A large shrub or small tree, this species has small, single, pink flowers. Blooms midseason. See Map 3.

**C. SALICIFOLIA:** Its small, single flowers are white and slightly fragrant. Leaves are long and narrow, and the plant's growth habit is low and bushy. It is a native of Hong Kong and Formosa. Blooms midseason. See Map 4.

**C. SALUENENSIS:** The small, single flowers of this native of southern China are white flushed with light to deep pink. Blooms mid- to late season. See Map 4.

**C. SASANQUA:** This native of southern Japan and the Ryukyu Islands has white to pink flowers. It is a large shrub or small tree. Blooms early. See Map 3.

**C. SINENSIS:** The commercial tea plant of Asia, this is a large shrub or small tree with small, white, single flowers. The medium, upright plants are generally hardier than *C. japonica*. Blooms midseason. See Map 4.

**C. TRANSNOKENSIS:** This slow-growing shrub has very small, single, white flowers. Its leaves are small and narrow, and the growth habit is narrow and upright. Blooms late. See Map 4.

**C. TSAII:** A native of southern China, *C. tsaii* grows as a shrub or small tree. It has small, single, white flowers and slender, waxy leaves. Blooms midseason. See Map 4.

**C. × VERNALIS:** The origin of this species is unknown; it is found only as a garden plant. It is very similar to *C. sasanqua*, but it blooms later. See Map 3.

**C. YUHSIENENSIS:** The very small, fragrant, single, white flowers bloom in great profusion. Blooms midseason. See Map 4.

# Ackerman Hybrids

The new Ackerman hybrids classified as winter-hardy extend the camellia's considerable charms northward. These plants are hardy to –5° to –10° F. For the first year after transplanting, they need some winter protection from sun and wind. Spring planting is recommended in all but Zone 8 and warmer areas.

'Ice Follies'

## FALL-FLOWERING CULTIVARS

**ASHTON'S PRIDE:** Blooming from mid-November to December, this plant has 2⅝-inch, medium to pale pink flowers with single, six-notched, cupped petals. The 3-inch-long leaves are semiglossy and dark green. Plants are vigorous and spreading, growing 8 feet tall and 7 feet wide in 12 years. See Map 2.

**SNOW FLURRY:** From October to November, this floriferous plant has 3½-inch, white, peony-form flowers with 12 petals and 18 petaloids. Leaves are leathery, semiglossy, and medium green. Plants reach 7 feet tall and 7 feet wide in 14 years. See Map 2.

**WINTER'S BEAUTY:** In late December to January, this plant's hardy flower buds turn into glowing shell pink, full-peony-form flowers. They have 19 petals and 7 petaloids and are 3 inches wide. The dark green leaves are leathery. See Map 2.

**WINTER'S INTERLUDE:** Blooming from November to December, this plant has pink, anemone-form, 3-inch flowers with 12 petals, 16 petaloids, and no anthers. Leaves are leathery, glossy, and dark green with wavy margins. Plants grow to 8 feet tall and 4½ feet wide in 13 years. See Map 2.

**WINTER'S ROSE:** From October to November, this plant has shell pink, formal-double flowers with 28 petals. Leaves are 2¾ inches long, leathery, semiglossy, and very dark green. 'Winter's Rose' is slow growing, to 6½ feet tall by 4 feet wide in 12 years. See Map 2.

**WINTER'S WATERLILY:** Blooming from November to December, 'Winter's Waterlily' has white, anemone-form to formal-double flowers with 21 petals and 15 petaloids. Leaves are 2½ inches long, leathery, semiglossy, and dark green. The shrub is a moderate grower, to 7 feet tall and 4½ feet wide in 12 years. See Map 2.

## SPRING-BLOOMING CULTIVARS

**FIRE 'N' ICE:** Blooming in late April, 'Fire 'n' Ice' has deep, dark red, 4-inch, semidouble to anemone-form flowers with red and white

petaloids and thick yellow stamens. It has average, upright, dense growth. See Map 3.

**ICE FOLLIES:** From March to April, this plant has medium rose-pink, large (4 inches wide by 2 inches high) flowers with 12 petals and six large petaloids. Leaves are dark green, and the growth habit is open and spreading. See Map 3.

**JERRY HILL:** The flowers are 3½ inches long by 3¾ inches wide, rose-pink, and formal-double. The leaves are dark green and 3¾ inches long. The plant habit is upright and dense. See Map 3.

**SPRING FRILL:** In March to April, 'Spring Frill' produces bright, iridescent pink, large to very large, semidouble to rose-form blossoms. The plant has a slow, spreading growth habit. See Map 3.

**SPRING'S PROMISE:** Wide, semiglossy, dark green leaves set off single, 2- to 2½-inch red-rose blossoms. The elegant petals radiate from a center of contrasting golden stamens. 'Spring's Promise' blooms from January to March. It grows 6 to 8 feet tall by 4 to 6 feet wide. See Map 3.

'Spring's Promise'

# INDEX

A number in boldface indicates
a photograph or illustration.

## PLANT INDEX

# THE USDA PLANT HARDINESS ZONE MAP OF NORTH AMERICA

Plants are classified according to the amount of cold weather they can handle. For example, a plant listed as hardy to Zone 6 will survive a winter in which the temperature drops to –10° F.

Warm weather also influences whether a plant will survive in your region. Although this map does not address heat hardiness, in general, if a range of hardiness zones are listed for a plant, the plant will survive winter in the coldest zone as well as tolerate the heat of the warmest zone.

To use this map, find the location of your community, then match the color band marking that area to the zone key at left.

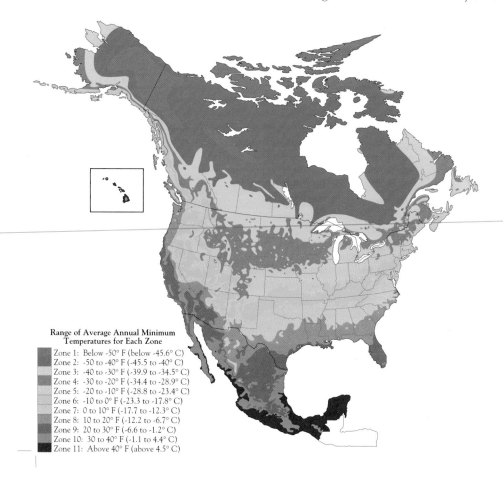

**Range of Average Annual Minimum Temperatures for Each Zone**

Zone 1: Below -50° F (below -45.6° C)
Zone 2: -50 to -40° F (-45.5 to -40° C)
Zone 3: -40 to -30° F (-39.9 to -34.5° C)
Zone 4: -30 to -20° F (-34.4 to -28.9° C)
Zone 5: -20 to -10° F (-28.8 to -23.4° C)
Zone 6: -10 to 0° F (-23.3 to -17.8° C)
Zone 7: 0 to 10° F (-17.7 to -12.3° C)
Zone 8: 10 to 20° F (-12.2 to -6.7° C)
Zone 9: 20 to 30° F (-6.6 to -1.2° C)
Zone 10: 30 to 40° F (-1.1 to 4.4° C)
Zone 11: Above 40° F (above 4.5° C)

## METRIC CONVERSIONS

| U.S. Units to Metric Equivalents | | | Metric Units to U.S. Equivalents | | |
| --- | --- | --- | --- | --- | --- |
| To Convert From | Multiply By | To Get | To Convert From | Multiply By | To Get |
| Inches | 25.4 | Millimeters | Millimeters | 0.0394 | Inches |
| Inches | 2.54 | Centimeters | Centimeters | 0.3937 | Inches |
| Feet | 30.48 | Centimeters | Centimeters | 0.0328 | Feet |
| Feet | 0.3048 | Meters | Meters | 3.2808 | Feet |
| Yards | 0.9144 | Meters | Meters | 1.0936 | Yards |

To convert from degrees Fahrenheit (F) to degrees Celsius (C), first subtract 32, then multiply by 5/9.

To convert from degrees Celsius to degrees Fahrenheit, multiply by 9/5, then add 32.